"CLUNE'S MEMOIRS WILL TAKE OVER YOUR BRAIN."*

"Unconventionally plotted and oddly moving . . . *Gamelife* argues that our hidden inner world, 'the part of our lives that wasn't involved with people,' can save us in an outside world that doesn't always make us feel whole."
—ETHAN GILSDORF, *The New York Times Book Review*

"Clune's book shows just how intense and intimate the engagement with video games can be . . . The book moves in counterpoint, alternating in short subchapters between exterior and interior, life and game, letting the two halves of Clune's experience jostle against each other in unexpected ways."
—GABRIEL WINSLOW-YOST, *The New York Review of Books*

"I never played the games Clune devotes most of his attention to . . . but his voice brings their obsolete rituals alive: Sometimes he sounds like a thriller writer, sometimes an art critic, sometimes a poet."
—CHRISTIAN LORENTZEN, *Vulture*

Is this a b[...]
? Yes

Is this fiction
? Error

Is this a memoir about computer games
? Yes

Is this by Michael W. Clune
? Yes

GAMELIFE

"Clune's memoirs . . . will make you *more* human, by doubling down on your capacity for empathy, as the best literature tends to do. They will leech compassion from your center and radiate it out through your pores, where you will worry others will see it and stare. These are books you should read if you're interested in being alive on earth." —*IAN BOGOST, *Los Angeles Review of Books*

Farrar, Straus and Giroux www.fsgbooks.com

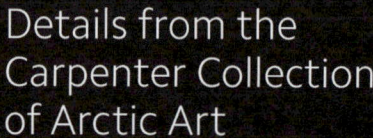

New from **University of Toronto Press**

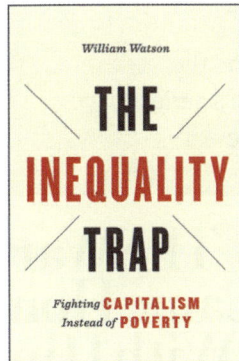
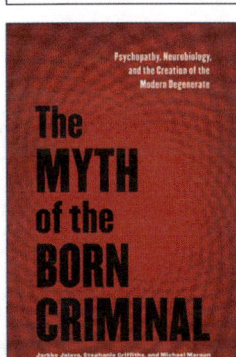
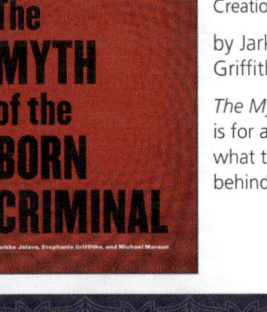

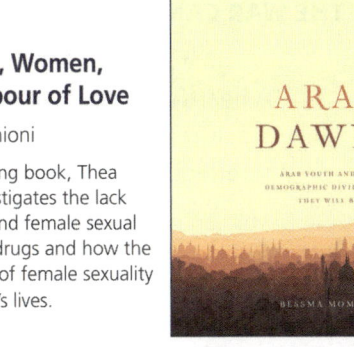

MORE THAN MEETS THE EYE

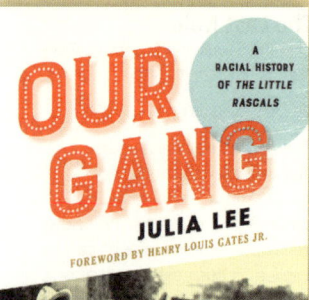

OUR GANG
Julia Lee
Foreword by Henry Louis Gates Jr.

A look behind the scenes of *The Little Rascals* and the America that made them to show how much this series reveals about black and white American culture— on either side of the silver screen.

$24.95 paperback | 336 pages | 48 b&w images

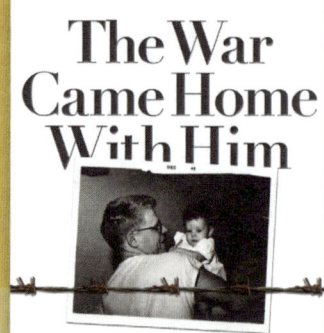

THE WAR CAME HOME WITH HIM
Catherine Madison

"A heartfelt account of a family fractured by war and its awful aftereffects." —*KIRKUS REVIEWS*

$24.95 paperback | 256 pages

DIABOLIQUES
Jules Barbey d'Aurevilly
Translated by Raymond N. MacKenzie

A masterpiece of French decadent fiction that combines horror, comedy, and irony to explore the foibles of aristocratic men and women.

$18.95 paperback | 336 pages

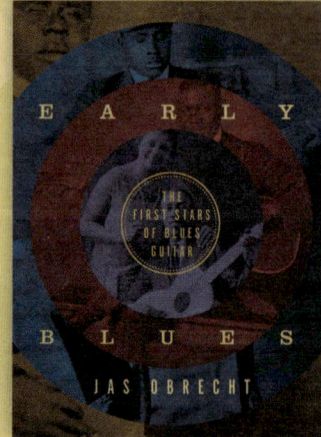

EARLY BLUES
Jas Obrecht

"Obrecht offers material that will be new even to readers who have been familiar with this music for many years." —**JIM O'NEAL,** founding co-editor, *Living Blues* magazine

$22.95 paperback | 272 pages | 70 b&w photos

 **University of Minnesota Press**
To order call 800-621-2736 *www.upress.umn.edu*

LOS ANGELES REVIEW OF BOOKS QUARTERLY JOURNAL | FALL 2015

EDITOR-IN-CHIEF
TOM LUTZ

EXECUTIVE AND QUARTERLY EDITOR
JONATHAN HAHN

SENIOR EDITORS
MIKE GOETZMAN, DINAH LENNEY,
MICHAEL URSELL, LAURIE WINER, KATE WOLF

POETRY EDITOR
ELIZABETH METZGER

CONTRIBUTING EDITORS
MERVE EMRE, SARAH MESLE, CALEB SMITH

ART DIRECTORS
MEGAN COTTS, MATT SIEGLE

PUBLICATION DESIGN
ELIZABETH KNAFO

ART CONTRIBUTORS
FRANK BENSON, ANDREA BOWERS, CHARLES GAINES, BILL JACOBSON,
JOSH MANNIS, ANNA MAYER, CARRIE MAE WEEMS

PRODUCTION AND COPY DESK CHIEF
WALTER HEYMANN

BUSINESS AND DEVELOPMENT
JESSICA KUBINEC

BOARD OF DIRECTORS
ALBERT LITEWKA, CHAIRMAN; REZA ASLAN, BILL BENENSON, LEO BRAUDY,
BERT DEIXLER, MATT GALSOR, ANNE GERMANACOS, SETH GREENLAND,
ERIC LAX, TOM LUTZ (EX OFFICIO), SUSAN MORSE, CAROL POLAKOFF,
JON WIENER, JAMIE WOLF

COVER ART
ANDREA BOWERS
MEMORY OF THE PARIS COMMUNE REVISED TO EQUAL WORK DESERVES EQUAL PAY,
(ILLUSTRATION BY WALTER CRANE), 2013
MARKER ON FOUND CARDBOARD
164 X 117" COURTESY OF THE ARTIST AND SUSANNE VIELMETTER LOS ANGELES PROJECTS
PHOTO: ROBERT WEDEMEYER

CHARLES GAINES
NUMBERS AND TREES III 'SHUCKS' #11, 1987
ACRYLIC SHEET, ACRYLIC PAINT, INK AND MASONITE; 50 1/2 x 42"
COURTESY OF THE ARTIST AND SUSANNE VIELMETTER LOS ANGELES PROJECTS; PHOTO: ROBERT WEDEMEYER

NYUPRESS
Keep reading.

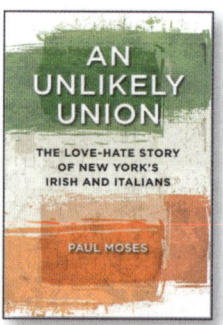

An Unlikely Union
The Love-Hate Story of New York's Irish and Italians

PAUL MOSES

"Alluringly explores how the two groups assimilated from separate tracks and on occasion inevitably collided."

- New York Times -

$35.00 • CLOTH

Surveillance Cinema

CATHERINE ZIMMER

"[A] genuinely groundbreaking study."

- Times Literary Supplement -

$27.00 • PAPER

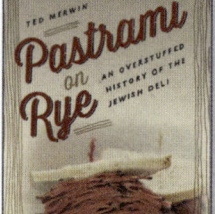

Pastrami on Rye
An Overstuffed History of the Jewish Deli

TED MERWIN

"[An] affable dive into the culture and history of the Jewish deli."

- New York Times Book Review -

$26.95 • CLOTH

Not Gay
Sex between Straight White Men

JANE WARD

"Fundamentally sound and refreshing...Greater understanding of any cultural phenomenon is only a good thing for the world."

- Gawker.com -

$25.00 • PAPER

Modern Families
Stories of Extraordinary Journeys to Kinship

JOSHUA GAMSON
FOREWORD BY MELISSA HARRIS-PERRY

"This beautifully constructed...hilarious manifesto rings with hope."

- Andrew Solomon - author of Far from the Tree

$26.95 • CLOTH

Is There Life After Football?
Surviving the NFL

JAMES A. HOLSTEIN, RICHARD S. JONES, AND GEORGE E. KOONCE, JR.

"[T]he information and insights engage in a rousing race for the end zone."

- Kirkus Reviews -

$27.95 • CLOTH

This Muslim American Life
Dispatches from the War on Terror

MOUSTAFA BAYOUMI

"Fascinating...This engrossing book challenges the entrenched...stereotypes about Arabs and Muslims."

- Nader Entessar - Library Journal

$19.95 • PAPER

Dissent
The History of an American Idea

RALPH YOUNG

"Convincingly demonstrates...'protest is one of the consummate expressions of Americanness'"

- Publishers Weekly - Starred Review

$39.95 • CLOTH

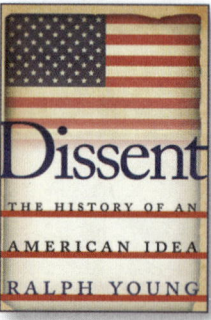

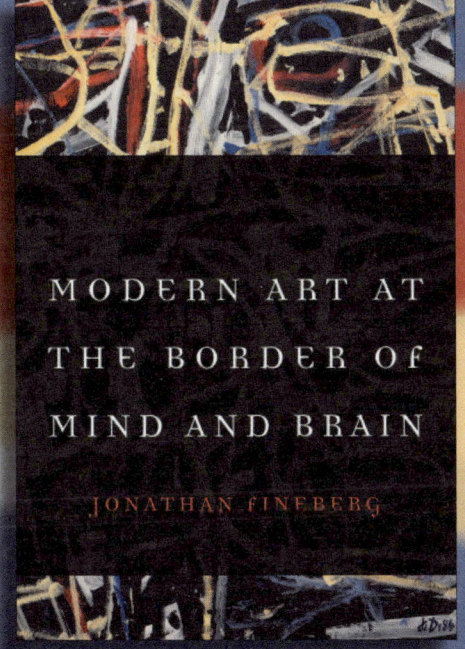

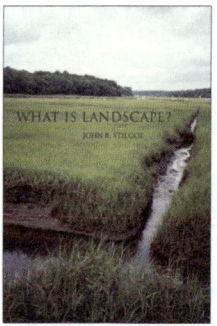

WHAT IS LANDSCAPE?

John R. Stilgoe

"Weaving together long-lost lore, etymological esoterica, and astute observations on ongoing developments, Stilgoe challenges common assumptions and imbues overlooked environments with unheralded significance."

—**Timothy Davis**, National Park Service, Landscape Historian

Hardcover | $19.95 | £13.95

MAKE IT NEW

The History of Silicon Valley Design

Barry M. Katz
foreword by John Maeda

"Beneath an engaging narrative lies a carefully researched and theoretically grounded understanding of the critical role that design has come to play in the world's most dynamic center of innovation."

—**Ikujiro Nonaka**, Hitotsubashi University

Hardcover | $29.95 | £20.95

A PREHISTORY OF THE CLOUD

Tung-Hui Hu

"Before we dismantle the cloud in our fight against the centralization of power, it's crucial to know its history. Thanks to Tung-Hui Hu's excellent book, we now do."
—**Geert Lovink**, media theorist

Hardcover | $25 | £17.95

SOUND ART

Sound as a Medium of Art
edited by Peter Weibel

Essays and images that map art's new sonic cosmos, illustrated in color throughout.

Copublished with ZKM | Center for Art and Media, Karlsruhe | Hardcover | $60 | £41.95

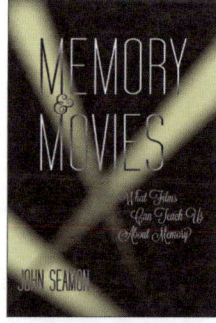

MEMORY AND MOVIES

What Films Can Teach Us about Memory

John Seamon

"Sometimes movies get the science right, sometimes they don't (and sometimes it doesn't matter). In this book, John Seamon connects science to art in a way that advances both—and suggests new themes and plots for future directors."

—**John F. Kihlstrom**, University of California, Berkeley

Hardcover | $29.95 | £20.95

OBFUSCATION

A User's Guide for Privacy and Protest

Finn Brunton and Helen Nissenbaum

"This important book is essential for anyone trying to understand why people resist and challenge tech norms, including policymakers, engineers, and users of technology."

—**danah boyd**, author of *It's Complicated: The Social Lives of Networked Teens* and founder of Data & Society

Hardcover | $19.95 | £13.95

NSK FROM KAPITAL TO CAPITAL

—Neue Slowenische Kunst—
AN EVENT OF THE FINAL DECADE OF YUGOSLAVIA

edited by Zdenka Badovinac, Eda Čufer, and Anthony Gardner

The generously illustrated, lavishly documented story of NSK (Neue Slowenische Kunst), one of the most significant art collectives of the late twentieth century. Each individual copy is printed with a custom detail; no two covers are exactly the same.

Paperback | $49.95 | £34.95

JOSH MANNIS
WHAT CONSTITUTES HUMAN EXCELLENCE?, 2015
INK ON PAPER, 25 1/2 x 22"
COURTESY OF THE ARTIST

Contents

Unwrap a world of ideas.

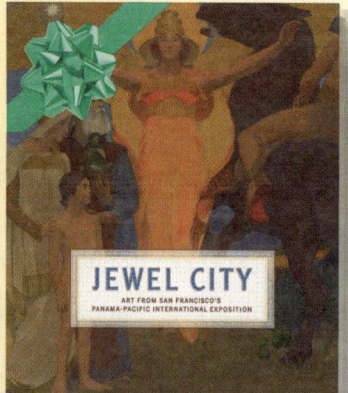

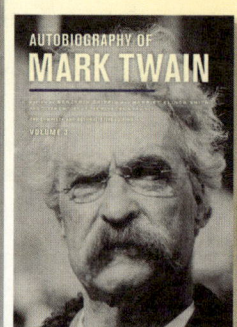

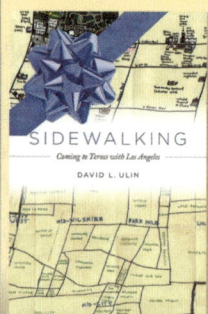

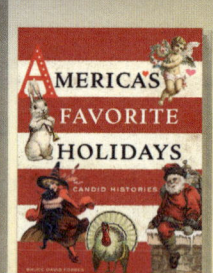

FEED YOUR HEAD

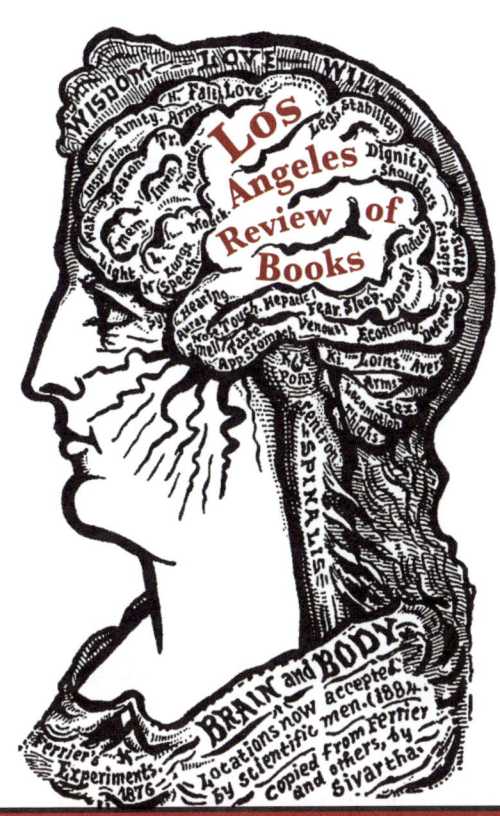

Join LARB's sustaining membership program today.

We are a nonprofit member-supported literary magazine, publishing daily online and distributing print publications like the one you are holding now.

Learn more at:
lareviewofbooks.org/membership

INTRODUCING "NO CRISIS"

MERVE EMRE, SARAH MESLE, AND CALEB SMITH

IT IS HARD TO MAKE A LIVING in criticism these days, yet there are some of us who can hardly imagine living without it. Too often, we have heard that we are living in an era of "crisis in the humanities," traditionally the home of the interpretive disciplines. This is not untrue exactly. Across the systems of education in the United States there are, in fact, many crises. But there are also strange polemics in the air. We — critics, scholars, writers, artists — are accused of having lost touch with the classics; of making the wrong political commitments; of producing ugly, jargon-ridden writing. We are accused of bringing the crisis on ourselves. Those who attack us, on both the left and the right, often say that they would prefer to save or defend some truer version of the humanities. But their bad-faith attacks end up justifying budget cuts, hiring freezes, class cancellations, program closures, and other austerity measures. For our part, we see the crisis as the effect of economic and administrative decisions, not a failure of ideas.

In "No Crisis," we consider the situation of critical thinking and writing in the 21st century, and we hope to show that the art of criticism is flourishing, rich with intellectual power and sustaining beauty, in hard times. Here was our plan: We got in touch with a group of eminent critics and writers from a range of institutional settings, working on various topics. Several of them were tenured professors; some were not. A few were not academics at all, but each had written pieces that moved or provoked us. We told them that we wanted to introduce readers beyond the academy to some of the best recent criticism. To that end, we asked each of them to choose a recent critical text and to write about why it mattered. The idea, we said, was not coolly to describe and evaluate, as in a book review; it was to stand with and think alongside a critic whose writing the contributor valued. This value, we said, could be intellectual, social, emotional; the tone of the essays could be personal, playful, or more conventionally serious.

One of our aims for the series was to account for how criticism is actually written in the present, to consider the state of the art, but we did not wish to put forward a manifesto or ask our contributors to sign on to a program. We had no interest in pronouncing the death of an old school or inaugurating a new one. We wanted the account to emerge more spontaneously — a collage-like picture, composed of many points of view.

Still, a couple of patterns, frequencies of tone and mood, might be perceived across the essays we have brought together in this volume. One is a drift away from the fantasy that our intellectual work, whether we call it criticism or that spikier name "critique," could ever stand outside systems of inequality or coercion, untouched by them. In many of the essays, there is a feeling of deep entanglement and impurity — "a recognition of complicity," as Johanna Drucker puts it in her piece on art historian T. J. Clark's *Farewell to an Idea*. Evan Calder Williams makes the point even more forcefully when he asks whether an academic or critic, particularly one who lacks job security, should "be asked to soldier on [...] because one cares, because one loves it, rather than because one is paid." One thing that may have been lost in the crisis is the institutional autonomy that allowed some critics to imagine that they could speak truth to power without, at the same time, speaking with and within power. There is no more noncomplicity. As Tavia Nyong'o shows us by way of the conceptual artist Adrian Piper, critics must learn to "live in this present experimentally" somewhere between the "emancipatory and constrictive" realities of the world — and critique, in turn, must become a little less saintly, a little dirtier.

A related pattern, another kind of impurity in the "No Crisis" essays, is an effort to reconcile an oppositional politics and an openness to beauty. This is what Peter Coviello admires so much in Jennifer Doyle's writing about the arts — the way she "stages a vibrant encounter between [...] fury and love," and what Jonathan Freedman finds in his study of love in Eric Lott's *Love and Theft* — that love is "as full of ambivalence, rage, will-to-power as it is of tenderness, joy, and exaltation." Maybe loving your object of study, taking joy in its mysteries and its weird gorgeousness, doesn't have to be some leisure-time indulgence, set aside when you turn to the serious business of unmasking or historicizing. Maybe, as Namwali Serpell proclaims in her essay on Rita Felski's *Uses of Literature*, there is no contradiction between analysis and attachment. Maybe, as Kathryn Bond Stockton speculates, reading and interpreting are themselves a mode of physical, even sexual, intimacy. Maybe the capacity for delight, for affiliation, can animate critical work, all the way through.

Indeed, the most thrilling moments in "No Crisis" often come from the rediscovery of life through criticism, in ways both small and large. Michael Clune's childhood memory of pretending that the raindrops on windows were gun sights takes on new meaning after Rei Terada teaches him to think differently about ephemeral perceptions. Kenneth Goldsmith's essay unfurls an account of how the 20th-century art critic Vilém Flusser has helped him reimagine the digital production of the 21st. Lauren Berlant's critical work prompts Virginia Jackson to consider the emotional thorniness of romance — not only as a literary genre, but also as a desire we wake up to in the morning and a source of disappointment we confront at night. Kenneth Warren's confession that, as a college student, he felt he "lacked the intellectual background and the lived experience to [...] write real literature" opens onto a trenchant reflection on the relations between higher education, class consolidation, and race; Diana Fuss's meditations on memory, death, and aging ask us to imagine what modes of the human can be compassed by "the humanities." If "No Crisis" ends up promoting any kind of model for good criticism, it is one that is equal parts interpretation and intimacy.

The essays in "No Crisis" are works of criticism in their own right, showing how a sophisticated understanding might be sustained, not diminished, by a kind of love, which is also a form of shelter. ⁄

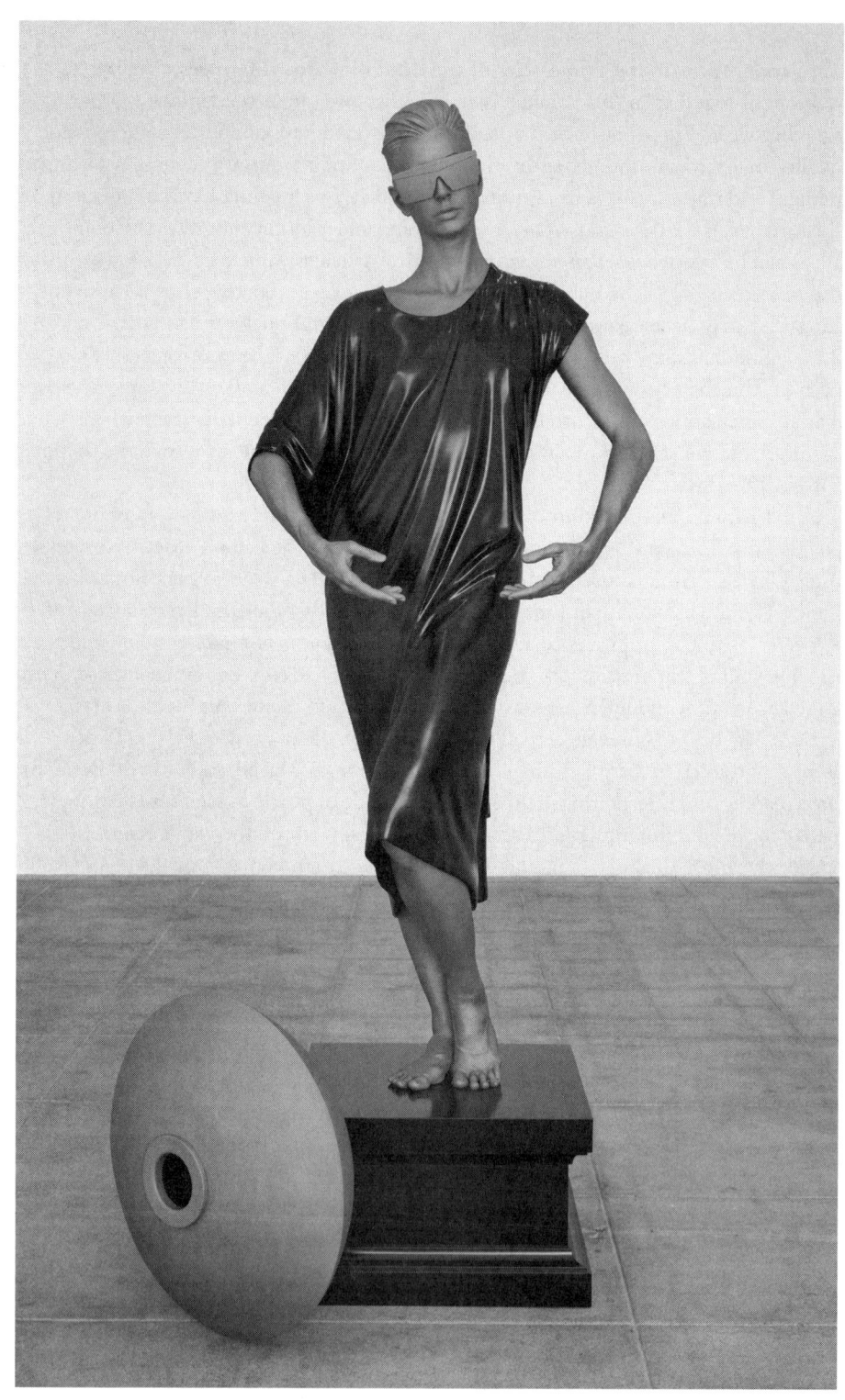

FRANK BENSON
HUMAN STATUE (JESSIE), 2011
BRONZE, MARBLE; 79 1/4 x 12 1/2 x 20"
COURTESY OF THE ARTIST AND ANDREW KREPS GALLERY, NEW YORK

USES OF CRITICISM

NAMWALI SERPELL

RITA FELSKI describes her remarkable work of criticism, *Uses of Literature*, as an "odd manifesto as manifestos go," an "un-manifesto," and "a defective or delinquent manifesto." It might seem that Felski protests too much. But she is simply trying to accommodate a nuanced book to a boldly titled series, Blackwell Manifestos, in which "major critics make timely interventions to address important concepts and subjects." The series description stipulates that its texts be "written accessibly and with verve and spirit" and "engage and challenge the broadest range of readers […] interested in ongoing debates and controversies in the humanities and social sciences." The prompt for this review of Felski's manifesto, part of the *LARB* series called "No Crisis," has a similar impetus behind it. I was asked "to choose a critical text from the last 15 years or so, and to write about why it matters. The idea is not coolly to describe and evaluate, as in a conventional review; it is to stand with and think with a critic whose writing you value." One reason I selected *Uses of Literature* among the various recent critical texts I admire is because it is a key, and sometimes overlooked, origin point for the very energy and motivation behind something like "No Crisis," the editors of which say: "we hope to express some of the beauties and pleasures that we find in criticism now." This is precisely the task Felski sets for her 162-page text, except that she hopes to find beauty and pleasure in literature and film rather than criticism.

It might seem odd to call a goal so familiar and positive — so beautiful and pleasurable — a "manifesto." Felski notes that while her book suits one definitional aspect of the form — a harping on one note — it also eschews the avant-garde legacy of the manifesto as a demolition of art, history, and value. This is why *Uses of Literature* is an un-manifesto, "a negation of a negation, an act of yea-saying not nay-saying, a thought experiment that seeks to advocate, not denigrate." To say yea in the aftermath of a recent critical and theoretical tradition so inclined to naysay is indeed a battle cry. This is how Felski describes the current doldrums of the discipline:

We are called on to adopt poses of analytical detachment, critical vigilance, guarded suspicion; humanities scholars suffer from a terminal case of irony, driven by the uncontrollable urge to put everything in scare quotes. Problematizing, interrogating, and subverting are the default options, the deeply grooved patterns of contemporary thought. "Critical reading" is the holy grail of literary studies, endlessly invoked in mission statements, graduation speeches, and conversations with deans, a slogan that peremptorily assigns all value to the act of reading and none to the objects read.

Following the lead of Eve Sedgwick, Felski notes that this posturing lends itself especially well to what Paul Ricoeur dubbed a "hermeneutics of suspicion." Felski castigates this as

a quintessentially paranoid style of critical engagement [that] calls for constant vigilance, reading against the grain, assuming the worst-case scenario and then rediscovering its own gloomy prognosis in every text. [...] [C]ritics find themselves unable to justify such readings except by imputing to these works an intent to subvert, interrogate, or disrupt that mirrors their own. The negative has become inescapably, overbearingly, normative.

The editors of a 2009 special issue of the critical journal *Representations,* Stephen Best and Sharon Marcus, offer a similar assessment of the field, while taking up Sedgwick's call for a new mode of reading. The set of essays in the issue exemplify what Marcus and Best term "surface reading," which they see as a counter to the tendency to dig beneath the text's surface that Felski also bemoans. This *Representations* issue has been widely addressed, cited, and refuted; there have been calls for papers and at least one conference devoted to the topic. Perhaps because Felski's book came out just the year before, it is not mentioned in the issue and has received slightly less attention. Felski would not necessarily have been the right fit for the issue. As she has elsewhere noted more recently, "the general idea of 'reading for the surface' has been around for a number of decades" in poststructuralist criticism influenced by Foucault and Barthes, and it does not necessarily solve the problem of suspicious reading because it is equally susceptible to a "hyper-vigilant, über-critical sensibility." Criticism that "stands back" to examine the text's surface is still keen to "denaturalize" that surface, is still "imbued with the spirit of disenchantment, the difference being that the diagnosis of illusions no longer culminates in a retrieval of buried secrets."

Rather than turning to surface, as such, Felski stakes her claim in *Uses of Literature* for what she calls a "neo-phenomenology" of reading, "thick descriptions of experiential states," which toggle between surface and depth, cognition and affect, lay and scholarly reading, literature and life. While the history of phenomenology in philosophy is of less interest to her, using a theory of experiential knowledge as a general heuristic appeals for several reasons. It attends to the first-person perspective; it calls us "back to the things themselves" and analogously to "do justice to how readers respond to the words they encounter"; it permits a catholic approach to a spectrum of literary responses; it accounts for "milieu and moment," as well as the "densely woven filters of interpretation and affective orientation" built into reading; and finally, it permits an unapologetic focus on the everyday, the commonsensical, the quotidian, and the pragmatic — hence the unapologetic titular word "uses." As she puts it:

To propose that the meaning of literature lies in its use is to open up for investigation a vast terrain of practices, expectations, emotions, hopes, dreams, and interpretations — a terrain that is, in William James's words, "multitudinous beyond imagination, tangled, muddy, painful and perplexed."

This phenomenological bent also links Felski's work both to the feminist criticism in which she was already a pioneer, and to recent returns to "affect," "aesthetics," and "ethics" in the discipline at large. The greater freedom of the manifesto form allows Felski to consider a plenitude of texts — poems, novels, plays, and films — that exemplify oft-denigrated ways of engaging with literature: *recognition, enchantment, knowledge*, and *shock*. She separates these four "modes of textual engagement" into a "tentative taxonomy," while acknowledging that they are neither exhaustive nor mutually exclusive; her conclusion goes some way toward articulating their interplay.

Chapter one opens up the question, "What does it mean to recognize oneself in a book?" via several scenes of recognition *within* literature, whereby characters discover themselves — their thoughts, their desires — in the novels they read. While critics have long been wary of the "Madame Bovary" problem, Felski attributes the recent scholarly trepidation about recognition to two factors: the fetish for alterity in studies influenced by philosopher Emmanuel Levinas, and the impact of critical theory's two key scenes of misrecognition, Jacques Lacan's essay on the mirror stage and Louis Althusser's description of hailing as an ideological apparatus. Noting that the "idea of misrecognition presumes and enfolds its antithesis" — that is, recognition — Felski goes on to point out the far more positive uses of recognition in fields like politics, anthropology, and sociology. Recognition in these contexts, she argues, conjoins knowledge (of the self) and acknowledgment (by others); subjectivity becomes inextricable from intersubjectivity. Felski's readings of the reception of Henrik Ibsen's *Hedda Gabler* and reception within Pankaj Mishra's *The Romantics* reveal recognition's capacities for *self-intensification*, awareness that one's experiences are distinctive but not unique, and for *self-extension*, seeing oneself in what initially seems strange. A brief discussion of Virginia Woolf's description of Mrs. Ramsay's "wedge-shaped core of darkness" in *To the Lighthouse* offers the possibility that what we recognize in literature is precisely what is opaque in all of us.

In chapter two, Felski takes up another bugbear of ideologically minded criticism: *enchantment*. She begins with a brilliant juxtaposition of, again, meta-scenes of aesthetic engagement: literary critic Joseph Boone's rapturous close reading of modernist novels and actress Mia Farrow's face as she watches the movies in *The Purple Rose of Cairo*. Alternating between the scenes reveals just how spurious is the distinction between the "fastidious attention to the luminous aesthetic detail" in close reading and the "all-embracing sense of being swept up into another world" in film-going. Both, after all, involve "total absorption in a text, of intense and enigmatic pleasure," that "confounds our deeply held beliefs about the rationality and autonomy of persons." Felski draws attention throughout this chapter to the anachronistic feel of enchantment, which seems to lead us right back to primitive, childish, or nostalgic ways of experiencing art. But this rejection of enchantment — as old as Plato's casting the poets out of the Republic — is often attended by various forms of snootiness: classism, iconophobia, and sexism. Deconstruction and cultural studies both evince a condescension toward feminine, "low" artifacts of enchantment. Felski recovers its uses in an anime film, Miyazaki's *Spirited Away*; Manuel Puig's play *Kiss of the Spider Woman*; Charles Bernstein's poem/essay "Artifice of Absorption"; and several works of criticism including J. Hillis Miller's *On Literature* and D.A. Miller's *Jane Austen, or The Secret of Style*. Each of these texts presents the necessarily dual nature of "modern enchantment," an awareness of the bounds of time and mediation around the enchanted moment. As Felski paraphrases Michael Saler, the contemporary "ironic imagination" entails "a pleasure in enchanted worlds that simultaneously acknowledges the imaginary nature of such worlds." This duality allows us to consider enchantment's absorptive, somatic effects without acceding entirely to its ideological sway.

Chapter three offers a strenuous critique of the bad faith that characterizes literary criticism's tendency to dismiss literary *knowledge*. Criticism, Felski points out, relies on the very same truth claims it critiques in so-called naive readings of literature. It also often treats mimesis as a straw man, ignoring its complexity or holding it to impossible standards of utter fidelity and comprehensiveness in representing the world. While criticism does take literary knowledge into account, it too often relegates it to a set of symptoms; in this model, the text does not know what it knows — it unwittingly enacts or displays the deep structure of ideology lurking beneath its surface. Felski argues that these critical moves avoid key aspects of mimesis: its inextricability from genre, which enables its most transparent effects; its inextricability from artifice, which is precisely what grants literature a heightened and often unprecedented access to experiential truths; its ineluctable mediation, which in fact does mirror the ineluctable mediation of experience itself; and its capacity to refer beyond itself, if not necessarily to the real world. Felski relies heavily in this chapter on Paul Ricoeur's notion of mimesis as metaphor (rather than as reflection), and takes up his description of how the world is *prefigured* by discourse, and how the literary text then *configures* this material, and thereby *transfigures* the reader. Felski articulates the phenomenological knowledge that literature makes available through three mimetic devices. She unfolds the intersubjectivity — the mind reading — that renders Edith Wharton's *House of Mirth* a "social phenomenology." Tim Winton's Australian novel *Cloudstreet* exemplifies the ventriloquy literature affords, while honing the political edge to a well-worn critical celebration of heteroglossia. And Pablo Neruda's *Residence* poems allow Felski access to literature's material knowledge, the wondrous attention to objects that opens up a tactile, textural, yet textual phenomenology of everyday things.

Felski concludes *Uses of Literature* with the mode of engagement most popular in our current critical environment: *shock*. She presents here a crucial counterpoint to the generally positive aesthetic bent she has thus far shown. Yet, as she demonstrates, aesthetic theory across several disciplinary lines has continued to reject the "shocking" in order to privilege affects like empathy or intellectual capacities like disinterestedness. Even those critics who have self-consciously addressed shocking material, like Fredric Jameson or Leo Bersani, tend to domesticate these texts by placing them firmly within the past, logical frameworks, or predetermined logics like psychoanalytic disturbance and linguistic *différance*. This taming, Felski points out, characterizes the history of the avant-garde's shock tactics, which were always both asocial and deeply social, possessed of bravado and theatricality as well as genuine utopian violence. Despite claims to the contrary, shock is always mediated; it simply cannot entail the complete dissolution of self or cognition. Rather than glibly mapping eruptive art onto revolutionary history, Felski considers texts that have stayed — or become — shocking to us, including Euripides's *The Bacchae*, Heinrich von Kleist's *Penthesilea*, Charles Baudelaire's "Une Charogne," and Gayl Jones's *Eva's Man*. These texts prove her contentions about the odd temporality of shock: its refusal to adhere to a teleology whereby we become less shockable; its tendency toward punctuation and suddenness; its part in the surprise-habituation-surprise spiral of literary history; its susceptibility to contextual contingency; and crucially, its exemplarity for *afterwardness*, a larger scale historical version of the time lag inherent to the psychoanalytic patient's experience of trauma. This chapter also showcases Felski's skills as a feminist critic, as she acutely assesses the gender dynamics of shock (often masculinist attempts to offend feminine prudery), while drawing attention to a "shadow history" of shock in the female "novel of sensation." She concludes by meditating on two perpetual threats to the shocking text: the audience's indifference or its absolute refusal.

In these four short chapters, Felski goes a long way toward recuperating familiar reading responses that have lately been given cursory or cavalier treatment in critical study, that have been deemed gullible, rationalist, reactionary, or totalizing. To consider the values of literary experience in this broader way undermines the dichotomy between high and low art. Felski seeks out examples of "emphatic experience," a framework capacious enough to encompass a panoply of aesthetic encounters, as well as "the differential force and intensity" and "multiple value frameworks" they afford. The risk of the positive aesthetics she "rough(s) out" in these pages is that ever-present threat to the critic: seeming naive. Is it possible, she asks, "to discuss the value of literature without falling into truisms and platitudes, sentimentality and *Schwärmerei*?"

Yes, I would answer: *Uses of Literature* proves it. By way of conclusion, I'll posit that Felski avoids losing this "gamble," this "quixotic wager," because of her deft deployment of four modes of *critical* engagement. These *uses of criticism*, so to speak, are oriented toward phenomenology — the experience of reading Rita Felski. They are neither exhaustive nor mutually exclusive; they do not correspond exactly to Felski's modes, nor do they roll off the tongue quite as well as hers. But they blend, in Felski's words, "analysis and attachment, criticism and love." I call them *mediation, modulation, redescription,* and *wonder*.

Throughout *Uses of Criticism*, Felski attends to the *mediated* nature of aesthetic engagement at different levels. By mediation, I mean both attention to medium — to the forms that filter artistic communication — and the lay sense of diplomatic intervention. Mediation of the first kind broadly characterizes Felski's phenomenology; she adopts Ricoeur's effort to reframe phenomenology as "the interpretation of symbols rather than the intuition of essences, as well as his insistence that the self is always already another, formed at its core through the mediating force of stories, metaphors, myths and images." This allows Felski to render her mode of *recognition*, for example, far more complex than the homilies about identification and "relatability" that get tossed around academic circles and the blogosphere. To recognize oneself in a text is a "perplexing and paradoxical" thing: "in a mobile interplay of exteriority and interiority, something that exists outside of me inspires a revised or altered sense of who I am." Felski also never loses sight of the mediation endemic to art as such: "aesthetic pleasure is never unmediated or intrinsic." In her chapter on *knowledge*, language does not preclude access to "truth," it structures it: "knowledge and genre are inescapably intertwined, if only because all forms of knowing — whether poetic or political, exquisitely lyrical or numbingly matter-of-fact — rely on an array of formal resources, stylistic conventions, and conceptual schemata."

These brilliant interventions about mediation are a kind of lens — or perhaps the pixelated view through the weave of a veil — that Felski inserts into the critical camera we train on art. This attention to medium is important because the modes of response Felski considers are frequently derided for ignoring or eliding literary form. As she paraphrases the critic Marie-Laure Ryan's thoughts on *enchantment*, "readers are so entirely caught up in what they are reading that the verbal medium is effaced: they no longer perceive or register the words they are scanning, but feel themselves to be fully subsumed with an imagined world." And yet, as Felski points out, Ryan fails to consider "the possibility of being seduced by a style," "the possibility of an emotional, even erotic cathexis onto the sounds and surfaces of words. Here language is not a hurdle to be vaulted over in the pursuit of pleasure, but the essential means to achieving it."

In this smart engagement with Ryan, we see not only Felski's keen eye for literary texture, but also an example of her deft mediation between different schools of critical thought. The sheer range of references on display in *Uses of Literature* necessitates some of her maneuvering between the Scylla and Charybdis of, say, deconstructive and cultural criticism, or ideological and theological critique. Felski has a wonderful ability to treat other critics with respect while noting their shortcomings; she raises an eyebrow at critics who denounce using literature for knowledge only to wield truth claims left and right, or who insist on the "radically asocial and disruptive aspects of shock" while achieving great "success in making a career of writing about it." Mediation characterizes Felski's negotiation of textual exempla as well, as she moves with great dexterity between high and low genres, between canon and candy. This form of mediation, in a diplomatic sense, is quite distinct from that tendency toward overqualification that marks — and mars — so many literary critics. Felski may perpetually move between persons, ideas, texts, but she does so with boldness and clarity.

Her refusal to be pinned down — or to put it more positively, this openness toward variance as a principle of selection and argument — suffuses her attunement to the vicissitudes of time, as well. I'd categorize this as Felski's use of a critical mode of *modulation*. This works at a micro-level, as when she describes shock's relationship to suddenness,

> a violent rupture of continuity and coherence, as time is definitively and dramatically rent asunder into a "before" and "after" […] a distinctive temporality characterized by a logic of punctuation, as the continuum of experience shatters into disconnected segments marked by dramatic variations of intensity.

But it also works at a macro-level, as when she considers how *Nachträglichkeit*, or afterwardness, affects the enigmas of textual transmission:

> Thanks to this time-lag between the occurrence of an event and its resonance, meaning is delayed, washed forward into the future rather than anchored in one defining moment. And even as fragments of past experience persist into the present, their meaning mutates under the pressure of new insight. Retrospection recreates the past even as it retrieves it, in a mutual contamination and commingling of different times.

Felski's phenomenology also takes advantage of modularity in forms other than movement through time. Felski's use of a loosely modular structure — her four "modes of textual engagement" — offered a template for my first book, *Seven Modes of Uncertainty*, reviving the taxonomic impulse of old-school critics like William Empson while allowing categories to bleed into each other. In her individual chapters, Felski sees *knowledge* and *recognition* as related concepts, and uses *enchantment* and *shock* as foils for one another. In her conclusion, she discusses the relationship between *knowledge* and *enchantment*, alludes to the notion of a shock of recognition, and deconstructs the opposition between *shock* and *enchantment* by showing that the former can be alluring and the latter can be disturbingly uncanny. By calling her four logics of aesthetic reception "modes," Felski can meditate on their aesthetic, affective, and ethical energies. Modulation also allows for the variation among readers, within readers, and in the dramatic fluctuations that characterize individual reading experiences, with their multiplicity of motives and affects, strategies and scenes.

This might seem too much like a series of crumbling boxes stuffed with ragtag exempla if it weren't for Felski's intense and detailed descriptions, which I call a mode of *redescription* in accordance with her own preference for the term elsewhere. While a hermeneutics of suspicion tends to dissect and pierce textual exempla, a countermethod of mere surface description begs the question. As Tzvetan Todorov put it in his introduction to *The Fantastic*,

> Literature says what it alone can say. When the critic has said everything in his power
> about a literary text, he has still said nothing; for the very existence of literature implies
> that it cannot be replaced by non-literature. [...] If descriptive science claimed to
> speak *the* truth, it would contradict its reason for being.

Rather than eschewing description, Felski doubles down on it, so to speak, the reasoning for which is somewhat analogous to her choice of the word "recognition" over "identification": "when we recognize something, we literally 'know it again'" and yet "recognition is not repetition; it denotes not just the previously known, but the becoming known." Redescription, in Felski's hands, becomes an adroit tool for bringing into being an already mediated experience, be it reality or reading.

Sometimes this entails breathing spirit into texts that I have not read. Of *Cloudstreet*, she writes,

> It is not far-fetched to think of language as another dwelling place in the novel, as a force
> that shelters and gathers together its inhabitants. Its bricks and mortar are colloquialisms,
> slang, vulgarities, Australianisms, passing observations and clichés, assembled into a shape
> of experience that is both familiar and strange.

Of Neruda's paean to "prodigious scissors," Felski lucidly evokes how "entangled in human lives, companionable if calmly indifferent, such daily things serve as precious repositories of associations and memories, marked with the traces and smells of their users, bearing witness to an infinity of accumulated acts and untold histories." Very often Felski's redescription approaches defamiliarization — making us attend once more to what is right before our eyes:

> Scissors have cut their way through history, trimming nails, making flags, chopping
> off hair, cutting out cancers [...]. A mundane object turns out, on closer inspection, to
> be monumental in its sheer ubiquity, as indispensable as eyes or teeth, an astonishing
> prosthesis caught up in the endless symbolic and practical work of culture.

As Felski explains in her conclusion, one of her aims is to look "anew at what we have assured ourselves we already know."

But rather than simply making the familiar strange, *Uses of Literature* often recasts the familiar as *wondrous*. Felski performs for aesthetic experience the service for which she praises poetry: "its single-minded attention to the sheer thingness of the thing, which may paradoxically reanimate and revitalize it, saving it from the abyss of oblivion or obsolescence." The parts of Felski's book that I quoted at length in my own are the "thick descriptions of [the] experiential states" afforded by her four modes. These passages, often in the first or second person, are so vivid that I will simply quote some exemplary excerpts of what I would name a critical mode of *wonder*. Here is Felski:

> On *recognition*: While turning a page I am arrested by a compelling description, a constellation of events, a conversation between characters, an interior monologue. Suddenly and without warning, a flash of connection leaps across the gap between text and reader; an affinity or an attunement is brought to light. I may be looking for such a moment, or I may stumble on it haphazardly, startled by the prescience of a certain combination of words. In either case, I feel myself addressed, summoned, called into account; I cannot help seeing traces of myself in the pages I am reading.

> On *enchantment*: You exist only in the present and the numinous presence of a text. Not only your autonomy but your sense of agency is under siege. You have little control over your response; you turn the pages compulsively, you gaze fixedly at the screen like a sleepwalker. Descriptions of enchantment often pinpoint an arresting of motion, a sense of being transfixed, spellbound, unable to move, even as your mind is transported elsewhere. Time slows to a halt: you feel yourself caught in an eternal, unchanging present. Rather than having a sense of mastery over a text, you are at its mercy. You are sucked in, swept up, spirited away, you feel yourself enfolded in a blissful embrace. You are mesmerized, hypnotized, possessed. You strain to reassert yourself, but finally you give in, you stop struggling, you yield without a murmur.

> On *knowledge*: The technique of deep intersubjectivity instantiates a view of particular societies "from the inside"; we come to know something of what it feels like to be inside a particular habitus, to experience a world as self-evident, to bathe in the waters of a way of life. By attending to the salience of what is said and what is left "unsaid, by reading looks and gestures, attending to half-voiced thoughts and inchoate sensations, we become attuned to criteria of distinction that seem at first glance to be baffling or opaque, that may surprise us in their sheer arbitrariness. *The House of Mirth* does not just depict a network of social discriminations and judgments, it also enfolds readers, through its inculcation of countless examples, into an experiential familiarity with the logic of such judgments, with what we might call a "feel for the game."

> On *shock*: We are slowly made aware that the corpse is in a state of perpetual motion; maggots are pouring like a viscous liquid across the ragged remains of the body, falling and rising like a series of waves. The poet is struck by the sheer beauty of this rhythmic movement as it mimics the music of running water and the sound of the wind. Even as he conjures up the horror of death jerked back to life, of flesh uncannily animated by the worms that are consuming it, he wrenches us into an awareness of the remarkable symmetries that thrive in the midst of putrefaction. Yet this aestheticizing gaze does not

annul the horror of what is being evoked but accentuates it; the rotting carcass is both like, yet utterly unlike, the blossoming flower to which it is compared.

As the latter two evocations of Wharton and Baudelaire suggest, this mode of *wonder* — a kind of awe at the things literature uses us for — emerges not simply from a rhetoric of subjectivity or affective intensity, but from a close attention to what Felski calls the "grain and texture" of specific works of art. The texts she analyzes seep into her language, tilt and stretch her images. She thus evinces precisely the openness to art she advocates while intensifying *other* readers' experiences of the texts. These moments of wonder are not the bloodless abstractions of reader response Felski abjures in her introduction. They are rich phenomenological *redescriptions* that retrace aesthetic experiences as they *modulate* over time, as they expose the textural seams of their *mediation*.

These moments of redescription thus enact the closest thing to a slogan in Felski's book: "What literary studies sorely needs at this point is not just a micro-politics but a micro-aesthetics." Despite the bracing clarity and boldness of statements like this, I agree with Felski's hedging about the term "manifesto." As a neo-phenomenology of the "different, even incommensurable reasons" we value literature, as a testament to the fact that "there is no single fiber that runs through the entire thread of reader response," Felski's book lacks the blunt force of a manifesto, that blind strike *for* or *against*. No, it is not really a manifesto. Rather, and this is what I most admire about it, *Uses of Literature* epitomizes a most valuable use of criticism: it makes art itself manifest. ◢

from *LAND*

JULIE KANTOR

14)

From the distance looks so dark, & next to the
trees, in the blackness of their dense & black-
green we say, "we can stay right here, never go
anywhere different," laid out like a target w/rings
of rock types dipping away from the center, not
say sorry for it, drawn back into these hills always.
We stay on the same angular unconformity which
lets us know it's only a matter of time before this
gets more lopsided, one or the other both wanting
transport through fire-control, interact in complex
ways in trampling pressure, determine face of all
the land around us before we knew but now together
think it could be us in the rainshadow of higher
elevation wedged in southern edge, first to go
up, be over w/but keep all continuance ordered.

16)

Blanket rock ledge in chain link & that
will keep us protected as we drive past
in different cars & times on highways
that don't have lamp-lights at all & half-
blind take mountain curves, turn head-
lights off when we can feel the other turning
them off, too, & blasted at slabs, boulders,
pieces of earth carve pathways for hiding,
we don't have to be cut at every time
out is wanted. Say, "as long as we think
we know that we know we are each alive"
we'll be covered, & pay for mileages up
the sides of endless slopes upward
to split these masses into two parts:

//

AGAINST COMMON SENSE

MICHAEL W. CLUNE

LET'S BEGIN with an uncommon sensation. Early in Tao Lin's novel *Taipei*, the protagonist sees his girlfriend at the other end of a hallway.

> Paul, walking self-consciously toward her, vaguely remembered a night, early in their relationship, when he somehow hadn't expected her to enlarge in his vision as he approached where she'd stood (looking down at a flyer, one leg slightly bent) in Think Coffee. [He remembered] [t]he comical, bewildering fear — equally calming and surprising, amusing and foreboding — he'd felt as she rapidly and sort of ominously increased in size […].

By describing Paul's experience as uncommon, I don't mean that this kind of thing is rare. Such oddly minor cognitive or perceptual blips might be rare, but they might not be. At any rate, people tend not to talk about them. We may not even remember them; they seem to lack the kind of significance that would make them memorable.

For example, when I was young — and even not-so-young — I used to pretend the drops of rain on my parents' cars windscreen were gun sights. I would line up a passing object with a particular drop, and imagine that I was "shooting" it. I never spoke to anyone else about this, and probably would have forgotten it long ago. But one day a friend casually mentioned to me that *he* used to pretend raindrops were gun sights. As the years have passed I've come across two or three others who also admitted doing this.

Discovering I shared this with my friend didn't bring us closer together. Realizing we love the same movie, finding out we both volunteered for the same obscure leftist politician: these things bring us closer together. But not our strange way of looking at raindrops. It's not hard to see why.

Pretend, that upon reading Lin's example, you remember you'd had a similar experience. And pretend you tell a friend about it and they discover they'd also had it. Now imagine how the conversation would go:

"So let me get this straight. You saw someone who was far away. And then you, like, just sort of thought they'd just remain small when you walked toward them? Instead of getting bigger?"

"Exactly."

"Wow! I had the exact same experience one time."

"For real?"

"Yeah. I totally kind of thought they'd stay small!"

"But they didn't."

"No, right. They didn't. It was just a … a thing."

"Yeah."

[long silence]

Someone you "somehow" expect not to get larger as you approach, a raindrop you sometimes see as a gun sight: these just don't seem to be the kind of things we can have, in any robust sense, *in common*. Hannah Arendt writes that "to live together in the world means essentially that a world of things is between those who have it in common, as a table is located between those who sit around it; the world, like every in-between, relates and separates men at the same time."

Artworks, beliefs, city squares: these are common things, solid things, things that can be found in a community, things that people can hold in common. The quasi-perceptual blip that Lin describes isn't. It stands apart from the common world. Unlike religious visions or dreams or full-blown hallucinations, this experience seems to repel meaning.

And yet it nevertheless exerts a certain pull. It activates contradictory emotions. "Equally calming and surprising, amusing and foreboding." One finds occasional traces of its presence, distributed like blanks across social life in stray remarks. If Lin is right, drugs have lately been pulled into the service of this mysterious impulse. Drugs in his novel — Ambien, Xanax, Adderall — are machines for opening small departures from the perceptual norm that don't quite rise to the level of hallucination. His novel isn't anomalous. I've seen records of strange, minor perceptions that aren't exactly normal, and aren't exactly abnormal, in other artworks, ranging from Sigmar Polke's photography to Mei-mei Berssenbrugge's poetry.

What appears in these appearances? These apparitions fit so exactly into the space between the genuinely strange and the utterly quotidian, that space about which it's so hard to speak. What is the source of their fascination?

———

Rei Terada's 2009 book *Looking Away* explains why people have been fascinated by "particularly ephemeral perceptual experiences." She provides therapy for those who feel that their interest in these perceptions is childish, even shameful. The ephemeral experiences she studies include "afterimages of colors, double vision […], double-take […], and reflections taken as objects […], and as dramatic as flowers on the curtain that turn into faces," clouds taken for mountains, fireworks, looking at a landscape with one's eyes half-closed so that it appears underwater. All are instances of what she calls *mere appearance*. We are drawn to mere appearance "when we want to create distance between ourselves and the given world."

Terada excavates a philosophical tradition running from Plato through Kant, Coleridge, Nietzsche, and Adorno that links the emphasis on *appearance* with a vague, pervasive *dissatisfaction*. This association is easy for any of us to access. Imagine you're at a store. The register reads "$12.99," and you hand the clerk a 20-dollar bill. She picks it up, examines it, and says:

"This *appears* to be money."

How do you interpret this statement? On its surface, it's quite innocuous, trivial even. Roses are red, violets are blue, money looks like money. But by drawing attention to your money's appearance, the clerk opens a potential gap between what your money *looks* like and what it *actually is*. It is as if the clerk is withholding — or as Coleridge says, *suspending* — judgment about whether the piece of green paper in her hand is money. You might get the feeling that the clerk is not entirely satisfied with your money. You might get the sense that she is somehow *dissatisfied* with it.

"That's real money," you mutter angrily.
"Never said it wasn't," says the clerk, putting it into the drawer and counting out your change.

Imagine that as you leave the store you can't quite leave the scene behind. "This *appears* to be money." What the hell did she mean by that? That was real money you gave her. What's she trying to say? What's her problem?

This thought experiment shows that too great an interest in appearance is easily identifiable with a certain dissatisfaction. But perhaps the clerk's dissatisfaction isn't with your money in particular. Perhaps her dissatisfaction is both vaguer and more far-reaching. I vividly remember the time when I was 16 or 17 and I took out a 20-dollar bill, and thought — *this is just a piece of colored paper*. It felt as if the world was an iceberg that had just slid into the ocean.

Mere appearance, Terada writes, "is relief." It gives us the feeling "that something heavy is gone." Take out some money and look at it. Look at the way it *appears*. What is this appearance? The green papery appearance seems to cover or obscure its character as money. To see it as appearance is in some sense to refuse to see it as money. This is why the clerk's comment angers us. "That doesn't *look* like money," we want to reply, "it *is* money!" In this gap between looking and being Terada discovers a kind of freedom. We are momentarily freed from the necessity of recognizing the world.

Recognition, after all, entails a certain obligation. For one nation to recognize another is to accept it, to welcome it, to become obliged to address it in a certain manner. For a person to recognize the ex-lover who walks by is to register the claim he still makes. But to linger in "mere appearance" is to be free of the demands of recognition. Instead of a nation, you have something that looks like a nation; instead of your old lover you have someone who appears to be that person. Terada writes: "Instead of being like the skin of an object, […] appearance is the impression left when a belief is temporarily lifted away. What dissolves here is the obligation to endorse […] fact perception."

The example of money highlights the intertwining of value and fact that has troubled philosophy for generations. To recognize a fact is also to endow it with value; real things have a claim upon us that unreal things don't. We feel as if we must accept facts as soon as we recognize them as facts. As soon as the clerk recognizes the bill as money, she must accept it.

Drawing on post-Kantian philosophy, Terada marks a distinction between "object perception," when we attend to the appearance of a thing, and "fact perception," when we experience a thing as a fact embedded in the social world. Just as the clerk avoids depositing the bill so long as she examines its appearance, "lingering in object perception" enables one "to avoid the value entailments of fact." When we dwell in mere appearance, "the world feels lighter," and "the association of appearance with mereness, lightness, radiance, and hypothesis is our only way of registering the absence of a weight we carry without knowing it, the perceived pressure of the given world and its natural laws on our potential endorsement."

How does one dwell in appearance? By cultivating those impressions that seem, through their brevity and insignificance, perfect instances of *mere* appearance. The key is to be aware that what you are experiencing isn't a fact. To take one of Terada's examples, Coleridge knows that when he half-closes his eyes, and the landscape appears to be submerged under water, he isn't observing a fact. The land remains dry. Rather, he has framed his perception of the world in such a way as to enable it to float gently free of reality. "Casting a perception as mere appearance [...] allows the mind to entertain it without endorsing it." Similarly, by framing his experience of the girl in the hall by the expectation that she won't get larger as he comes nearer, Lin's protagonist suspends his perceptual contact with the given world.

More importantly, he suspends contact with the person whom he approaches. Attention to mere appearance, Terada writes, "becomes a way to get away, or imagine getting away, from other people." We turn "toward these perceptions to deflect the other's invasion, by the reasoning — the comically quick and amoral reasoning typical of the unconscious — that if the other is inexorable once perceived, then obviously one should put off perceiving it or not look straight on."

The sense that by attending to mere appearance one is avoiding others is one reason why the philosophers who have thought most deeply about aesthetics argue that "merely suspensive, illusory, or ephemeral perception" cannot be aesthetic. Part of the point of art, part of the defense of its value, has always been that it's socially affirmative. Art builds community. Kant, for instance, believes that we expect others to agree with our judgment of a landscape or painting as beautiful. This expectation demonstrates, in his influential view, our possession of a *common sense*, a common sense activated by aesthetic perception. He dismisses "ephemeral and indefinite perceptions" because he doesn't think we can expect others to share them. Or, Arendt might add, because their very flimsiness, their *mereness*, renders them unable to support a common world.

Adorno, unlike Kant, is suspicious of our common world. He suspects that the appearances of capitalist society veil malign power relationships. He imagines art as an occasion for exposing the emptiness of bourgeoisie society. The art he loves is theatrically functionless, "a thing that negates the world of things." And yet he too refuses to admit "ephemeral and indefinite perceptions," like the kind provided by firework displays, into the realm of the aesthetic. "Adorno," Terada points out, "prefers that the artwork be able to be mistaken for another fact among social facts." He wants artworks to have solidity and duration. His critique of capitalist common sense depends on monumental artworks that everyone can interpret in common.

Against this tradition, writers from Coleridge to Lin think the fleeting, transient perceptions they cultivate are art. These non-facts furnish the substance of some of the most important post-Romantic literature. Consider Proust's endless interest in the changing light on his bedroom walls, or Dickinson's image of a hummingbird as a "wheel of evanescence." We have lacked a theory of this substance, largely because we have lacked a way of recognizing the desire that animates it. Terada makes this desire recognizable. She turns it into a fact.

Here is the fact: Something is wrong with the world. There is a fundamental flaw in society. Relations between people seem to have something wrong with them. Something … off.

Sometimes, when I want to share something with you, I realize that my experience has an unsharable dimension. I realize that we encounter each other only by peering across the thick boundary of our social personas. I don't know how to fix this problem, but I don't like it. I can only meet other people on the terrain of a common world that seems too heavy, too alien, too uncomfortable, too cold. Sometimes I protest by looking away, by watching the part of my experience that none of you can touch.

We all know about the kind of problem Terada describes, even if we avoid talking about it. It doesn't seem worth talking about. And it doesn't seem worth talking about because it doesn't seem fixable. A revolution might fix a lot of things. But no imaginable transformation of society will fix this.

We might get a firmer grip on the problem by approaching it from a slightly different perspective. Contemporary philosophy discusses the problem of "mere appearance," of unsharable perceptions, in terms of "qualia." Qualia refers to the qualities of perception. A common example invites us to consider the "redness" of a red object, while bracketing any meaning or significance associated with the object. A prominent strain in the philosophy of mind affirms that qualia are "epiphenomenal." That is, these experiences of mere redness and the like have no effect on the world. If they were suddenly to disappear, if we were all to suddenly lose our capacity to experience qualia, then, according to David Chalmers's famous thought experiment, nothing at all would change. The common world would remain the same.

But one doesn't have to go as far as Chalmers. Consider the example of Coleridge, squinting his eyes to give the landscape a blurry, watery look. What does it mean to say we can't share this experience? I can squint my eyes in the same way, and experience the same blurry look. Yet Coleridge's visual experiment focuses so exclusively on *mere appearance* as to strip away any *meaning* from the experience. And meaning is the sharable part of an experience. This is why discovering other people who imagined rain droplets were gun sights didn't enhance my relationship with them, didn't lead to any meaningful or memorable conversations.

"Oh yes, I experienced that too."

We ultimately can't say much more about such experiences. What can you say about the redness of a red object?

"It looks red."

We know — or at least we think we know — that when someone tells us they see the color red, their words correspond to a certain experience. But almost nothing about that experience, beyond the bare registration of its existence, can be brought into the public world, the world between people.

Philosophers like Chalmers are interested in the metaphysical and epistemological dimensions of qualia. Is there a certain kind of knowledge that can only be accessed through the first-person perspective, and not the third-person perspective of science? What is the relation between qualia and the brain?

Terada, on the other hand, wants to know why people deliberately cultivate the experience of mere appearance. She wants to consider the desire that leads us to look away from the common world, and to dwell for a while with surfaces of soap bubbles, reflections in water, surfaces of clouds, with droplets of rain. She recognizes that sometimes we want to watch the persistent solidity of the world simply dissolve in the fine glitter of mere appearance.

Terada anticipates the anxiety that recognizing this desire triggers. She knows people will rush into the gap opened by the phenomenophiliac in looking away with political, social, and psychological diagnoses. Certain Marxists will suspect that the phenomenophiliac really suffers from an advanced case of generalized commodity disorder. Doesn't advertising teach us to just look at the surface? Terada is a victim of advertising!

Certain philosophers, following Stanley Cavell, will argue that the phenomenophiliac's intractable dissatisfaction with society is a denial of "the structural limitations of human communication." We can never look through another's eyes, we can never truly share experiences. This is just the way things are. Stop denying it, accept it!

But Terada affirms, mildly, simply, that those who choose to look away are not denying the limitations of the world. They just "don't like these limitations." She listens patiently to explanations that the desire for a basically different kind of world is an impossible, childish desire. "One may feel justified in having desires," she replies, "even when there is no possibility of fulfilling them […] the absence of a grammar for such feelings reflects […] deeply internalized, unfreedom."

Terada has given us a grammar for the feeling of wanting to escape from something unfixable. In so doing, she's provided us with a way of understanding and appreciating one of the basic tendencies of the art of our time. This is what great criticism does.

And it does something else. Terada defines a limit. In dwelling with mere appearance, she tells us, we turn away from the world and nothing else. We protest society's intractable barriers, without knowing how to surpass them.

The history of art moves forward by transcending such limits as Terada identifies. Her masterpiece of description is also a challenge to create a kind of art that her magnificent concepts will no longer be able to describe. We should leave her book wondering if there's something more to say about those raindrops on the windshield, about the face Paul somehow expects not to get bigger, more about the color red. ⁄⁄

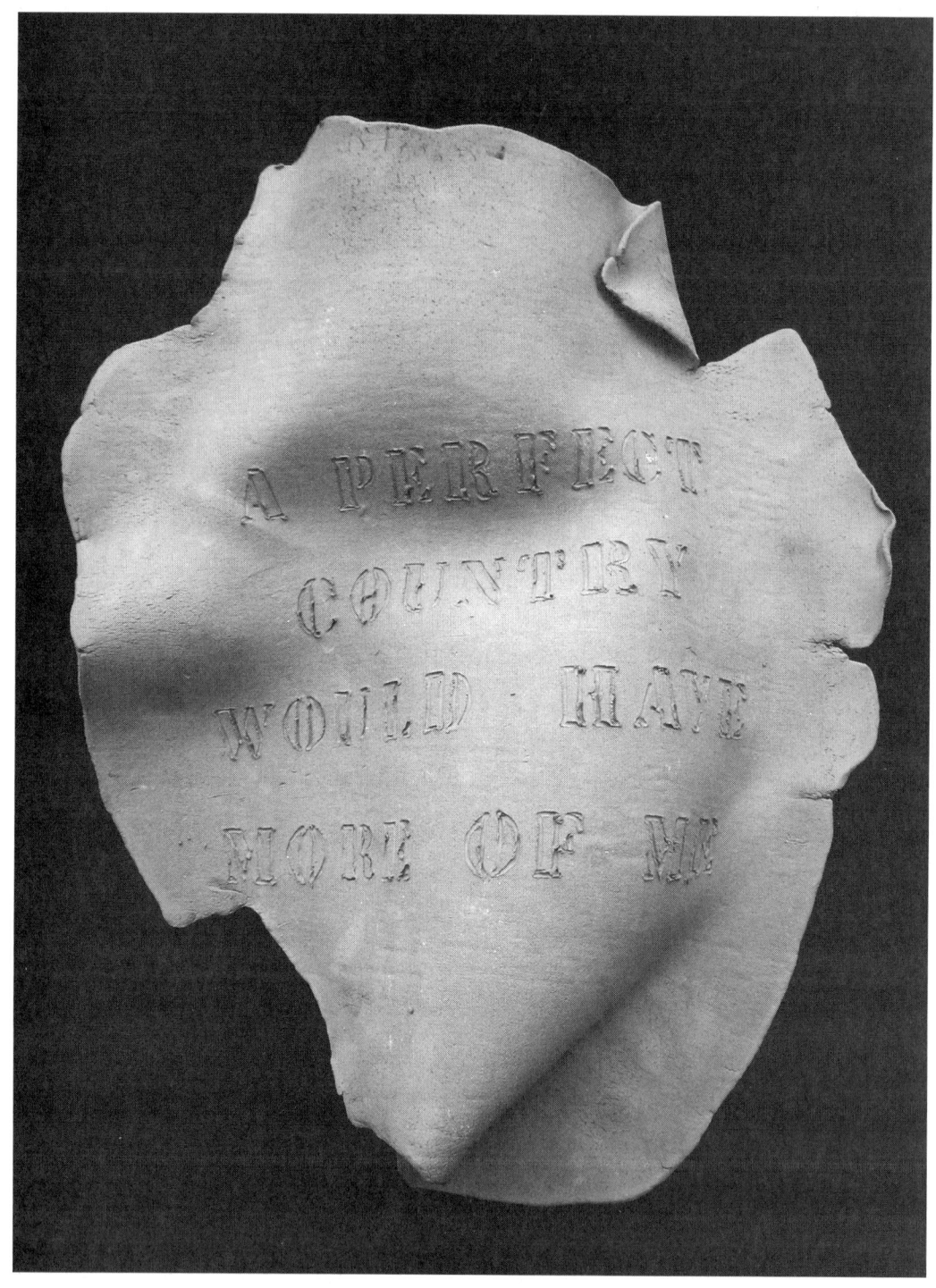

ANNA MAYER
A PERFECT COUNTRY WOULD HAVE MORE OF ME (ESCONDIDO CANYON),
FROM THE *FIREFUL OF FEAR* PROJECT, 2008–ONGOING
WILDFIRE-FIRED CERAMIC (FORTHCOMING), 18 1/2 x 15 x 3"
COURTESY OF THE ARTIST

The start of the free and natural

DOROTHEA LASKY

Dear friend you have a problem and it's called yourself
Dear self you have a problem and it's called yourself
Dear swamp demon you stole from me
Dear sky you have a night
The stars they go
Dear sun you have a problem and it's the light
Dear night you have a problem
I can't see anyone except the red music box
Dear love you see too much
I went to the wooden lake
I saw the wooden people
I took one out
It was a boy
It was wood and did not breathe
It had its wood hair grain
In a static wave
I breathed life into it
Its eyelids finally swung open
I told it it was once a tree
I laid it down I picked it up
Out its eyes came the clear liquid
But not tears, just humor
Just plastic utterances
Out its mouth came the words
But it wasn't alive yet
The stars in its absence, X-ed out
The middle sun, it shone
But only for me
Out your sink the bitter flowers
Oh, they have bloomed in the sewer
And the sewer flowers are jealous
Of what of what
How dare you ask
Obviously
The air ⁄⁄

DIFFICULT LOVE

PETER COVIELLO

BACK IN 2008, that *annus horribilis* of crisis and collapse, an art student at Yale conceived a project. Aliza Shvarts, for her senior thesis, undertook a "yearlong performance of repeated self-induced miscarriages." As Jennifer Doyle describes it in *Hold It Against Me: Difficulty and Emotion in Contemporary Art*, Shvarts "artificially inseminated herself over the course of nine months and took herbal abortifacients at the same point in her menstrual cycle in order to facilitate menstruation or miscarriage." The work itself, which was to include narrative and a documentary presentation, was disallowed presentation at Yale, in part because Shvarts refused to "confess in writing that the exhibition is a work of fiction," which is how Yale's publicists tried to spin the story once it became *Drudge Report* fodder. But the voices of chastisement were not only Drudge's. Here is the venerable Robert Storr, dean of the school of art at Yale: "If I had known about this, I would not have permitted it to go forward. This is not an acceptable project in a community where the consequences go beyond the individual who initiates the project and may even endanger that individual."

Some difficulty is good for us. And some, it seems, is not. *Hold It Against Me*, Doyle's incendiary and extravagantly rewarding book, isn't much interested either in celebrating the difficult as such — a move with a storied and, by now, unenlivening modernist history — or in equipping us with a more responsive taxonomic vocabulary for encountering work that resists us. "My aim," Doyle says early on, with something of the spark that characterizes the writing throughout, "is not to produce a reader who can point and declare, 'The difficulty of this performance belongs to category 4.'"

Instead, with larger ambitions in mind, Doyle's book organizes a series of far-reaching analytic case studies, and along the way stages a vibrant encounter between what I'd call, for short, fury and love. *Hold It Against Me* is a coruscating assault on the state of contemporary art critical practice, and especially on what Doyle reads, with demolishing exhaustiveness, as its genuinely outraging incapacity in relation to racially engaged, feminist, and queer art and artists. As Doyle reads it, this is a failure rooted in impoverished conceptual frameworks and broken institutional practices and lived out in encounters with individual artists and objects. You will not, I promise, emerge from this book with your sense of the conditions that mediate engagements with contemporary art, from the local to the mass-marketed, unshaken or unrevised.

And yet what energizes Doyle's critique, and makes the book the intensely vitalizing study I think it is, isn't so much its replenishing anger as the way that outrage is wedded throughout to a special kind of avidity, a special kind of *ardor*. If you are a person who spends a good deal of time around things like art, or books, or songs, you are likely to recognize in yourself some resonant echo of the feeling: I just mean the desire to bring an unflattened attentiveness, a suppler articulacy, to the scene of works you find provoking, captivating, involving in ways that fracture the terms of address that surround them. *Hold It Against Me* is a revelatory book of art criticism and politically astute theory. But I think it may also be a book about a certain mode of love — critical love — as counterhegemonic practice.

Among the most immediate inhibitions to rich articulacy Doyle finds in the vicinity of the work that interests her is the elaborate discursive machinery whose industry name is *controversy*. The case of Aliza Shvarts is exemplary in this respect but hardly singular. "Attention to a work's controversy," Doyle writes, "actually suppresses attention to a work's difficulty," and the pieces that she considers, when they aren't starved wholly for critical conversation from an institutional art world escalatingly wedded to salability as a paramount value, are instead warped and depleted by the idioms of controversy, made over into substantially less interesting versions of themselves. (The online organ *Jezebel* would helpfully describe Shvarts as an "avant-garde asshole.") Controversy locks us into a vision of the scene of art critique, and, as Doyle takes pains to show, it is by and large an awfully stupid one. Or rather, "controversy" is the language that an institutionalized nonresponsiveness habitually, almost reflexively, speaks. It gives us sides, establishes laws of "decency" and "taste," and aligns us with their maintenance or their overcoming. Whatever the works may have to offer outside of those frames — however they may batter themselves against exactly these conditioning parameters of reception — gets neatly invisibilized, though it does so under the sign of "engagement" or, still more dishearteningly, "debate." Doyle rightly wants no part of this game. Critics can do better than excoriate or defend, bury or praise.

At the heart of *Hold It Against Me* is the conviction that the works that most arrest Doyle's attention — by artists like Ron Athey, James Luna, Carrie Mae Weems, Nao Bustamante, David Wojnarowicz — have different sorts of stories to tell us, and that, for reasons that have everything to do with the state of art critical practice, we haven't yet figured out how to get them told. The works in question are, in the sense that Doyle specifies, difficult: by turns unnerving and alienating and disruptive, especially so in their solicitations and refusals, their troubling agitations, of emotion. Yet the challenge with which the book begins is not to some imagined viewer's brittle bourgeois sensibility. It is, instead, to critical appraisal itself, to *writing*. Early in the preface, Doyle writes, "This book describes the process of learning how to write about [...] work that feels emotionally sincere or real and that produces a dense field of affect around it even as it seems to dismantle the mechanisms through which emotion is produced." She goes on, in reference to works that she confesses had for years frustrated her efforts to write about them:

> All [...] are rich with affect, but none can be described as expressive in any traditional sense (none, in other words, can be explained as a representation of how the artist feels). All [...] feel political, but *why* they do is complicated. They are unnerving, depressing, or upsetting; none offers the positive message one associates with political art, and they each (differently) reject the basic geometries of identity and politics that normally ground discussions of art, identity, and politics.

If the work that most engages Doyle also frustrates her, this is in part because it keeps returning her to the scene of a certain vacancy, a meta-dispossession: it brings her again and again to the place where some apposite vocabulary from the archive of art critical thought *might* have appeared but, then, did not. It's art that, as Doyle encounters it, keeps yearning toward a critical apparatus that does not yet exist.

And so, leaguing herself with dissident critics like Lucy R. Lippard, Amelia Jones, Darby English, and José Muñoz, Doyle sets out to elaborate one. The book unfolds as a reckoning with the force of an unruly range of contemporary works but also, simultaneously, as an effort to build up around them a conceptual framework that might be adequate to their power and perplexity and vibrant, vibrantly *political* intricacy. It's here, too, that the most frontally polemical aspects of *Hold It Against Me* emerge. Because, as it turns out, to see what's at stake in Shvarts's unnerving suspension of affect around her staged abortions, or in Ron Athey's performances of bodily woundedness and extremity, or in Carrie Mae Weems's interruptive rescriptings of an archive of early photographs of African Americans, you have to disentangle them from a lot of accreted styles of knowing and seeing and talking. What this means, in *Hold It Against Me*, is that you have to be willing to take a torch to a good deal of what passes for critical engagement.

Prohibitions like Yale's, and the desultory effects of the language of controversy, are not, for Doyle, the only inhibitions to vigorous appraisal. "Critics have limits," she writes, and it's a generous note to strike at the outset, allowing as it does for differences of taste and tolerance and temperament. But the book goes on to anatomize what we might think of as the ideological implantation of those limits, and their nearly seamless naturalization under the sign of "emotion." In Shvarts's prohibited piece, for instance, much of what's revelatory to Doyle is the artist's "removal of sex from her project" — the way that, by "evacuat[ing] all traces of romance, love, and desire from the work," Shvarts tracks how rigidly abortion discourse "is shaped by both a guideline regarding *how one is supposed to feel* about the topic and a disavowal of the incoherence within our notions of the body and the subject" for which those feelings act as a kind of cover (my emphasis added). To think with and through the project at all is to "bear witness to the political difficulty of identifying abortion as necessary to the practice of sexual freedom," and to the specifically affective protocols that undergird that difficulty. It is to grapple with the ways feeling sutures not just a multitude of political investments but the field of "the political" as such, what gets to be counted *as* politics.

When Doyle comes to what it is that delimits the amplest responses to difficult work, the frame grows wider still. Taking cues from the work she admires and the styles of response (and non-response) that have gathered around them, and working with meticulous patience, she lays bare a great trove of tactics for ignoring, dismissing, derogating, misapprehending, or otherwise rendering marginal and mute the works of artists not understood to be "difficult" in the valorized ways (typically through austerity and abstraction) or "political" in the proper idioms. The problem isn't only the "flat-footed literalism" that routinely attends feminist and queer and racially marked art. ("From a patriarchal and defensive perspective," she writes, quoting Jane Blocker, "the 'female and the queer' body is 'not seen to be performing at all.'") The situation is more dire. "Outside of the writing of those scholars who are actively engaged with work by artists of color," she writes,

> art critical awareness of how artists mobilize and respond to racial discourse in their work is dismal. Few in the field of contemporary art history (generically defined) seem to read even canonical work on race, representation, and politics, and many of the voices most prominent in contemporary art history reinforce the curatorial isolation imposed on artists of color, ignoring whole movements in their attempts to identify and theorize the currents of the past few decades.

In this way a "deep suspicion of identity politics" among the most exalted of contemporary critics

CARRIE MAE WEEMS
YOU BECAME MAMMIE, MAMA, MOTHER & THEN, YES, CONFIDANT, HA, 1995-96
C-PRINT WITH SANDBLASTED TEXT ON GLASS, 26 1/2 X 22 3/4"
© CARRIE MAE WEEMS. COURTESY OF THE ARTIST AND JACK SHAINMAN GALLERY, NEW YORK.

yields to "a rather strange situation in art criticism in which the mere presence of especially race as an interpretive factor is enough to wipe out a work's difficulty and the complexity of its relationship to its context." Good luck, then, finding a ready-made analytic vocabulary with which to contend with the fine-grained emotional intensities that cluster around works fascinated less with "the liberal humanist's romance with his own racism" than with the entanglements of identification and dispossession — of blockage and impasse and fractured revelation, registered as turns of *feeling* — found at sites of historical trauma or excision.

So as Doyle walks us through Weems's *From Here I Saw What Happened and I Cried* — an installation of reproductions of early photographs of African Americans scored over by Weems's text — we do not merely see the institutional critique (of exclusion and fetishization, say) it is typically understood to perform, as it recodes the implicitly ethnographic gazes of 19th-century photography.

We find something more unsettling, something attuned more closely to the *affective* labors of race that travel beneath the surfaces of institutional efforts toward inclusion and restoration, often in ways that vanish as they approach the threshold of the articulable. Doyle shows us a work whose "emotional economy is organized around […] blockage; we are left with the feeling that something has happened, some kind of disaster, but we sense it only partially as a presence lurking behind the frozen expressions that greet the camera." Weems doesn't merely describe the pain of exclusion and fetishization, the Jamesonian "hurt" of any number of historical disasters. Instead she

> explores the poetics of depression, anger, and alienation that unfold around the moment America turns to specific communities when it needs permission to feel, in which the spectacle of one's reaction is always already working on behalf of someone, something else.

This is powerful, wonderfully responsive critical writing, but it's also more than that. It is analysis that takes its place as part of the book's larger effort to map out, encounter by encounter, "what it might mean to practice art history according to counterhegemonic models described by writers like Du Bois and Benjamin."

That's no mean ambition. And for my money, it is nowhere more movingly achieved than in the book's account of Ron Athey, and especially of his piece *Incorruptible Flesh: Dissociative Sparkle*. "In this work," Doyle writes,

> Athey lies on his back on a metal table made from scaffolding. […] His body rests against the fat metal rods of his platform for six hours. Built into the table is a pivoting rod, onto which Athey attached a baseball bat, upon which he has impaled himself. He is naked and covered in bronzing lotion and Vaseline. Hooks pierce multiple points in his face and are attached to leather strings to pull his skin back, turning his face into a painful (but also comic) mask. His scrotum is filled with fluid — turning his genitals into a watery, pink, feminine mass.

Doyle works through the performance with a layered attentiveness that, in the context of the scene itself, it's hard to think of as anything other than a mode of exquisite refracted care. Indeed, she writes that the "real show in this performance is not Athey's body but the spectacularization of our communal relationship to it," and this writing is in some measure an extension of it. The audience is welcome to put on gloves and touch Athey, so that the piece becomes a staging of care and its durational fluctuations of mood: how it might emerge as shame, tenderness, desire, boredom, humor, exhaustion. The piece may be gruesome and trying, and in its evocation of a queerly sexualized scene of immobilized endurance particularly resonant. But it is not, Doyle avers, "about AIDS in any traditional sense of that word *about*." It does not tell us an AIDS story about suffering, or care, or violation, or grief so much as it "absorbs us into the story's structure." I'll let her hard-won description stand:

> Athey not only exaggerates the social vulnerability of his body; he overtly eroticizes it. It's not mystical. It's a carnal refusal to turn one's eye to the heavens, an insistence on both *the magic and the banality* of flesh. It's what the body becomes under the disco ball's "dissociative sparkle," the weird and funny appeal of pearls pulled from his ass, or the

reveal of wounded flesh: the ordinariness of touch and the frank brutality of the nurse.
[My emphasis added]

You could love *Hold It Against Me* for passages like this alone, in which a mind as theoretically acute as Doyle's tunes itself to the fugitive inner dynamics of scenes so layered and fraught. And you could love it too for the elegance of its execution, its book-wide commitment to a critical language that is as companionable as it is exacting. And you could love as well Doyle's book-wide effort to *become* the critic these works seem to her to yearn toward: not to measure them according to some set of prior articulable political commitments but to learn from them, and from the modes of attention they induce, some suppler purchase on the dilemmas of the political as such. But there are other reasons, too.

I know a lot less about contemporary art practice than others might — it is certainly, for me, less a part of *how* to think through the world than it is for Doyle — but the work of *Hold It Against Me* feels near to me, intimately so, just the same. Like Doyle, and like many of you, I spend a lot of my time trying to figure out how to write about the things that agitate me into vehemence. Much of the pleasure of *Hold It Against Me* comes from getting to accompany a critic who is this kind of unembarrassedly engrossed by her objects, this kind of devoted to the under-described reach and consequence of them. For Doyle, this means doing a pitched kind of battle with the canonical underpinnings of her discipline — in this case, an art historical practice she finds to be wrought round with sexist and racist and homophobic presumption and proscription — because the authorized languages of that discipline make those works *harder to see*, to know or to address or to encounter in the breadth of their effects. Many of us, I think, know what this is like — know, I mean, the urge to shake the things we cherish loose of the frames in which they are found and in that way begin to make them legible to others, not necessarily as *better* than they might have been led to imagine, but as stranger, denser, brighter, and ampler, and more richly fucking *alive*.

Hold It Against Me is a commanding book of art history and critical theory, and I commend it to you on those grounds. But it's also an exemplary book about the intimacy of critique — of passionately antiracist and queer and feminist critique — and what we might as well call *love*. Doyle loves these objects, which doesn't mean she approves of them or "likes" them or thinks they're just awesome or needs you to know they're better than, say, something by Richard Serra or Matthew Barney. But it does mean that the necessity of changing the terms and the tenor of the conversation about them courses through the sentences of her book like electrical current. Much of the critical tradition teaches us to mistrust outrage, especially when coming from women, or queers, or people of color. Fury, we are told, makes a stone of the heart, and for that matter does not much make for edifying clarity. *Hold It Against Me* is without question an outraged book. (Reading it will make it hard for you to return to, say, the dilations of powerhouse art critical patriarchs like Dave Hickey or Peter Schjeldahl with anything but a swamping sense of their outrageous inadequacy.) But Doyle's book gives the lie to all such presumption, reminding us not only that hard political feelings can indeed make for penetrating clarity, but also that the misrecognized force that nourishes anger, that animates outrage, is, often, love.

And that, I think, makes *Hold It Against Me*, beyond its other field-specific virtues, a wonderful brief for the utility, the brightening edification, of love: for object-love, again, as counterhegemonic practice. It's true that for this formulation to work you have to understand "love" to comprehend not just gauzy delight but frustration and anger, as well as boredom, shame, curiosity and desire, sorrow and exhilaration, irritation and despair. But then, as anyone who's ever fallen for a difficult object knows — and critics are surely not alone in this beautiful affliction — it does. ◢

JOSH MANNIS
EVERY DAY COMES AND GOES, 2015
INK ON PAPER, 25 1/2 X 22"
COURTESY OF THE ARTIST

44

Babel / Constitution

LO KWA MEI-EN

After falling, an economy is taught to eject the body, to break
thee from you. This way to a surveillance where theorized horses

strain connectivity over the minor earth. I am ready to relay
crackling syrup from a radio tower. I am a tourist. War serves me

after fashion of lions cut up — gold behind and before — gunned by you
and yours away. I am rude yellow flies to summer's safety and

all lights blowing out domestic distribution. A zeroing of a bride,
chest of girly boudoir ammo, fling wide. Unpin me as I change

the costume's filament and rush the ginger middle like a sword
wanting deepness, tenderness. The tower settles. A hot porch wanting

more hive to harm. Thy lesson adds like water to be dammed.
Thy consequence kicks in, slips up, gets skinny in silk until hard

up goes the nation's head. Up, man, I learned thy name in a tower
kicking my feed of a god left feeding, his superhot-for-eros fruit

rolling back to the noise from whence it came till nothing called and
you came. The news pins a tongue on. A red light and claim that came

together last. A dumb nova of fathers, a rusted beast not waiting
for victims to avenge the lives of lips! If you had one face, horses

rung in steel could grow plain in the street. Or, freed of a name,
run into the yard of bridled lions, each an equation unbearable

and testing the light. ⁄⁄

READING AS KISSING,
SEX WITH IDEAS:
"LESBIAN" BAREBACKING?

KATHRYN BOND STOCKTON

YOU, TOO, SHALL BAREBACK

FIVE YEARS AGO, a treatise exploring barebacking practices hit academia with notable force. Readers professed themselves excited — and incited. And the book was lauded as bravery on the page, whether one views the phenomenon of barebacking as a thing to celebrate or to condemn.

Indeed, the back cover of Tim Dean's book, *Unlimited Intimacy: Reflections on the Subculture of Barebacking* (University of Chicago Press, 2009), describes his study as a "riveting investigation into [...] gay men['s] deliberately abandoning condoms and embracing erotic risk," a risk that may include contracting, or even seeking to contract, HIV. Martha Nussbaum, feminist philosopher and holder of an endowed chair in law and ethics at the University of Chicago, writes in her blurb: "*Unlimited Intimacy* is novel, fascinating, insightful, and courageous. Dean convincingly argues that confronting head-on a sexual subculture that is alien to most readers, and understanding the fantasies that propel it, is a very good way of stimulating thought." A second endorser, Matti Bunzl, of the University of Illinois, also seems stimulated: "This book does not break taboos; it shatters them. While many readers will come away from it with puzzlement, anger, and even disgust, it presents a compelling and entirely original analysis of the barebacking subculture."

A culture not so "sub," Dean informs us, as he offers readers neither manifesto nor apology, only a culture "with much to tell everyone — gay or straight — about how intimacy works in the twenty-first century." Or, in a nutshell: "Without going so far as to advocate for unprotected sex," Dean asserts, "I want to suggest that the [barebacking] subculture's embrace of risk may help illuminate the pleasures and ethics of encountering the unfamiliar."

Of course, on its surface, the idea of opening oneself to HIV, maybe seeking HIV, is truly unfamiliar to many readers (though surely not to all). But I can assure you, more unfamiliar, to almost any reader, will be the train of thought that I pursue here. The suggestion that readers, *by virtue of reading*, are "lesbian" barebackers, circa '09.[i]

Please read on. The pleasure of barebacking swiftly awaits you. And not as metaphorically as you might think. But let me mention another phenomenon, one that lurks around the edges of this essay, one you need not know too much about but explains my fascination with barebacking's focus on the *feel* of raw sex — sex without condoms (hence, the term "barebacking") — with its potentially risky penetrations and ingestions. It's enough to know that the essay you're reading is a fanciful engagement of the trend called "surface reading." The aim for surface-readers is not to be swamped by seeking "deeper" meanings such as your favorite deep-reading English teacher has sought. Rather, this phenomenon to which I'm responding calls for taking the surface of a text as a destination in its own right — almost at the level of one's just describing it closely, carefully, fully attentively. Take my essay as its own embrace of surface that would fondle depth.

Barebacking, reading: Each has a curious relationship to surfaces, signs, and depths. Each, for this reason, can be deemed "lesbian," strange as that may sound.

GETTING INSIDE US

Consider my central thesis, if you will. Receive it as it comes. Barebacking advertises (that's right, advertises) unprotected *reading* that I call "lesbian" and that our lives depend upon. Something's being advertised; something's unprotected; something's looking lesbian; something's giving life … that copulates with death. That thing is reading, and barebacking figures it.

Shall I put this yet more strangely? A lesbian quietly reading in the corner is like a barebacker chasing the virus. So is a lesbian kissing in the corner. Or make that a lesbian aggressively using a dildo in the corner. In fact, since these acts have historically come before barebacking practices, I would say the barebacker more resembles *them*. Gay male barebacking is like dildoing is like kissing is like reading: it's *a fetishizing of a sign and surface* that must get inside us, where a sign-and-surface birth and cause some death. In this way, barebacking figures those forms of reading that even children do — can't help but do, insofar as they read. Imagine a sleek, sexy campaign for Readers Are Leaders using barebacking as its hook.

Here, I get ahead of myself. To stay beside myself, to the side of myself, I want to kiss the "lesbian" sign in all of this. *It* may be the dildo, even the stranger, that needs to be your lover, birthing and breeding meanings inside of you. But let's get it straight: I am not a lesbian. I'm not even "homo." But I've made lesbians since I was a child. I can explain.

I AM NOT A "LESBIAN," BUT SIGN ME UP

I am not my girlfriend. We are not the same. Our genitals are different. Since mine are not hers, they are not the same. We use them differently; their use is not the same. I do things to pleasure her a man could also do — and if she closed her eyes, she might think I were he. If she always closed her eyes, she'd never know if he were me.

I'll sketch quickly our different ways of coming to what is called our sameness, a sameness undone by the ways we've come to it. The crucial point is this: we are each strangers to the sign "lesbian" and the sign estranges us each from ourselves. I was female-assigned at birth, though I thought I was a boy mistaken for a girl. And though I was to my mind the ultimate straight man seeking normally feminine women, I turned out a "lesbian," against my will — though in accord with my desires. As for my girlfriend, she grew up, to her mind, normally feminine, as a rural Mormon raised in rural Utah. In her 20s, after her male fiancé died, after she didn't go on a mission, after she walked across the US for nuclear disarmament, she met lesbians and wished she could be one, so cool did they seem to her. But she figured she wasn't a lesbian. Long story short: I didn't want the sign but was pierced by it; she quite wanted it but didn't think she'd gain it.

We have been dildoed by the sign "lesbian." We've been pleasured by it, as it's come inside us — I've had to try to take it like a man — but we've also split from each other at the very point of our contact with the sign. Somewhere where denotation births connotation, we start feeling erotic rips and tears. Ours is truly a fractured sameness in several directions. We are like the figure of two lips touching, touching *through* their gapping, that Luce Irigaray offered and explored in the 1970s as a figure for (self-) caressing through (self-) splitting (lips I wrote about in the 1990s as a figure for a sexual self-estrangement). Through our contact with the sign "lesbian," my lover and I, so profoundly different, touch upon the nearness Irigaray conceptualized through the touching lips, deriving pleasure "from what is so near that [we] cannot have it, nor have [ourselves]." Some self-fracturing, breaking sameness, is to be found in a "lesbian" kiss.

In fact, if there were time, we could rehearse how the sign "lesbian" has functioned historically as a bold estranging force, breeding estrangements with every use: Who is a lesbian? What do they do? Can it be sex? What is its continuum? Is it all dildo (only a sign of the missing penis that does the penetrating), or is it all kiss (surface relations of various sorts)? Sign and surface. Penetrating sign. Surface to be kissed. Hold these terms. And pivot with this:

The good old sexologists, from the 19th century into the 20th, didn't know what to do with "the femme." She was a stranger to lesbian desire. They tended thus to see her as a normal woman who was led astray by a "mannish lesbian." And I must confess, so delightful is the femme that I had a little game I devised in childhood to cheer myself up, whenever I was low, called "femmes at the mall." You know what I did: hit a shopping center and imagined that every appealing woman whom I deemed feminine was a femme lesbian, until proven otherwise. Since I never tested them, they were not disproven. And, therefore, due to this generous practice, the world was virtually — dare I say, virally? — full of lesbians, thanks to me.

All right, let's say you tentatively grant that the sign "lesbian" has bred estrangements, *advertised* estrangements, among both lovers and the broader public. What about gay male sex on this front? Could it be said to advertise anything? And why this curious word, after all: "advertise," of all things?

Another thinker can lead us on to Dean and, later, to the penetrating nature of reading, due to the ways in which reading is kissing. But, first, it may matter how we have sex with a certain idea: "sex" itself. Or with the climax taken for sex.

READING ORGASM (ANGRILY): ADVERTISING PENETRATION BY THE THOUGHT OF ORGASM

"Analysis, while necessary, may also be an indefensible luxury. [...]
[M]orally, the only necessary response to [public responses to AIDS] is rage."
— Leo Bersani, "Is the Rectum a Grave?"

So wrote the famous literary critic Leo Bersani in 1987, at the height of North American AIDS and during the dawning of queer studies. And so began, to my mind, a set of paradoxes that surrounds "doing" in queer domains, whether that doing is doing someone sexually or doing rageful politics. Analysis is somehow too luxurious, but also necessary; rage, furthermore, is not so much a violent feeling as deliberative *thought*, *outrageous* thought, making our action our rage against the state and the way it thinks. And against the ways gays and lesbians think. Action, for Bersani, is stopping "gay" thought. Something queer studies, in most of its varieties, has emphasized since.

What was the focus of Bersani's anger? First, displacement. Second, tumescence (of a certain sort). Bersani was enraged that the general public was displacing a health crisis — namely, AIDS — by treating it as a sexual threat. Also maddening was gays themselves wanting to redeem sex, to displace its self-disturbances, with something more self-enhancing in sex (like nurturance or love). In Bersani's view, what the state *and* many gays were taking from us — in trying to stamp out queer promiscuity in the time of AIDS — was the "radical disintegration and humiliation of the self" that come with orgasm's over-pleasure. Here's your estrangement force all right. Orgasm is pleasure, pushing into pain; hence, of course, for centuries orgasm has been called "a little death." It breaks the boundaries of a person's self, Bersani says, and he regards it as a positive, cleansing humiliation of one's selfhood.

Bersani was not content to point to the *unconscious* workings of orgasm that shatter selfhood and therefore resist easy, sentimental versions of "gayness." There were conscious actions of conscious thinking he wanted us to do, as if consciousness of what we were doing around self-fracturing made all the difference. Thus, I teasingly suggest that "Is the Rectum a Grave?" is Bersani's consciousness-raising piece: a genre straight out of lesbian feminism. Here, moreover, is what he pressed upon us, in his ardent anger:

— Consider that your self is not your friend: your very idea of your self is a kind of "psychic tumescence" that promises violence, since the harmful things you do are "in defense" of your sense of your self.

— Thus, he says, go get shattered. No, scratch that, if you're having sex you *are* getting shattered, just realize it: otherwise, you are repressing the fact that "sex [is] self-abolition."

— So, says Bersani, bury in the rectum your bad, proud selfhood.

See where I'm headed? What's paradoxical (and this is what I love) is how Bersani, who wants to ground his thoughts, unabashedly, in anatomical positions and the force of biological climax, ends up making orgasm something of a *metaphorical* penetration, something of a *sign*, an *idea*, we have sex with, before, during, or even after sex. Orgasm, if one follows his thought to its logical conclusion, is a figural penetration, even in acts that aren't penetrative (some oral sex, some digital sex, several kinds of "lesbian" sex). Everyone is penetrated/punctured/shattered no matter what they're doing, as long as they're coming. If I come, when I come, I am boldly shattered, making my orgasm the very "organ," to put it metaphorically, that penetrates me. Everyone's a catcher to orgasm's pitcher. Everyone's a bottom to their own climax. Everyone is punctured by the orgasm dildo. We are shattered by sensation but also (re-)invaginate sensation as a sign?

All this is intriguing in an essay, Bersani's, that wants us for a moment to be strictly literal when it comes to sex, that wants to combat our love of "displacements." And though Bersani may be anti-redemptive, famously so, he urges our pursuit of sex as "our primary practice of nonviolence" in contrast to relationship (which he sees as a battle of selves). Gay men especially can "advertise" this practice of sex as nonviolence.

("Advertise" is *his* word.) Why can they advertise? Because they are positioned, often through literal anal penetrations and promiscuities, to "represent the internalized phallic male [another sign, another idea?] as an infinitely loved object of sacrifice." Hence, gay men advertise orgasmic over-pleasure as (last Bersani phrase) "a mode of ascesis."

That's right, "ascesis" is the very last word of Bersani's essay. (Ascesis: the religious self-denial of monks and saints.) We exit his essay as ecstatic ascetics, whatever those are. St. Teresas, every one of us, if we have our consciousness raised? Picture the angel in Bernini's statue *The Ecstasy of Saint Teresa* holding a word/a sign/a surface rather than an arrow with which to pierce her entrails.

BAREBACKERS HAVING SEX WITH …?

If the barebacker likes his sex "raw," as they say, with no condom on, I suggest that two forms of fetish are at play: the feel of a surface (skin to skin) and the sign, the idea, of HIV. (Recall, for a moment, the dictionary definition of "fetish": something thought to have magical power; something to which one is irrationally devoted; something nonsexual with sexual resonance.) The fascinating aspect of this second fetish — HIV — is how it may function (think Bersani here) as a figural penetrator of *all* the parties present at a scene of penetration or semen-ingestion. If, at this scene, a sero-conversion to HIV-positive is possible for someone, whether or not anyone is seeking it, it's likely, though not certain, that HIV is a fetishized sign penetrating penetrator/penetrated/voyeur/or ingestor. The sign has gotten inside *any* body that is invoking it via speech or thought (consciously, unconsciously), whether or not the virus is actually getting "in" a body being opened up. Caressed by the mind, HIV can't be *felt* as anything other than a sign. Consent, nonetheless, happens at the surface, where one consents to begin a penetration or ingestion, where the *sign* HIV (and perhaps the virus) may be allowed to journey in the body in any number of invisible ways. At the very least, a commitment to a surface, its initial feel as a signifying force, is what penetrates those who are exchanging.

Then there's advertising. Tim Dean tells us that HIV "when pictured as bug-chasing" is an "attempt to coordinate birth and death, to make one's [sero-conversion] birthday the occasion for 'breeding' or initiating new [viral] life." Obviously, I'm implying that bug-chasing and barebacking (when they coincide — and sometimes when they don't) advertise one's kissing the sign HIV, letting it in, invaginating it through the anus or the mouth — and, of course, the mind — letting it do with you what it will: birthing something in you, letting something die, becoming a decaying of which you may not know the extent. And it seems certain, as Dean states: "the figure of the barebacker […] offers an image and an identity with which any gay man may flirt." Dean proceeds to add: "barebackers fuck without protection on behalf of those too timid to do so."

What's so sexy here? As Dean explains it, a "sacrificial ethos" reigns supreme. But here, masculinity, contra Bersani, is *shored up* by a man's "surviving […] physical ordeals, including multiple penetrations, humiliations, piercings, […] brandings, and infections." "Being HIV," Dean continues, "is like having a war wound or battle scar" — something "cognate with other physical tests that are necessary to constitute a heroic masculinity of almost mythic dimensions." What's happened here to Bersani's notion of the "internalized phallic male as an infinitely loved object of sacrifice"? Is barebacking advertising "self-abolition" or "psychic tumescence"? Is it in need of a "lesbian" puncture?

Whatever the answer, Dean, though never speaking of advertising, does discuss how cruising — seeking sex with strangers — "allegorizes" an "ethic of openness to alterity." And I must say, as he explains this allegorical ethics, I start hearing echoes of Irigaray (advocating "nearness" through self-splitting and self-estrangement: deriving pleasure "from what is so near that [we] cannot have it, nor have [ourselves]"). Cruising, says Dean, involves "how one treats the other and, more specifically, how one treats his or her own otherness"; "encountering a stranger brings one into contact with the unconscious."

There are even "lesbian" echoes here. Sounding a bit like Marilyn Frye in her famous essay "Lesbian Sex," where she argues that lesbian sex cannot be conceptualized according to standard notions of orgasmic climax or genital intercourse, Dean underscores that "the ethics of cruising" is not "reducible to genital satisfaction." Indeed, as a reviewer of Dean's book puts it: "the pleasure[s] barebacking subculture seeks […] are far more varied and [far more] diffuse than sex as sex is conventionally defined."[ii] Hence, there are no adequate measuring devices for the frequency of barebacking sex — a point Frye makes for "lesbian sex." And the sex that is "had," Dean emphasizes, is distanced from heteronormative *and* gay understandings. Ditto dyke sex.

Will the real estrangement force stand up?

Oh, that's easy. That would be reading, which the acts of barebacking, which I'm deeming lesbian, crucially figure. Talk about kissing a signifying surface …

THIS WORD WHICH IS NOT ONE: DILDO AND VIRUS

Reading is promiscuous, penetrating, pleasurable, vibrant, viral, and estranging, while it's rational somewhere at its core. Perhaps because it's cognitive, and can feel familiar, we can disavow the basic scandal and danger of reading, never mind its corporeal nature. And its transports.

Let me put "reading" as queerly as I can. In the act of reading, we are being penetrated by an author's sequencing of sensuous dildos we call words, which we kiss, which then open us up to viral growth (a growth that needs our bodies and what our brains supply). The word is a dildo? A dildo we kiss? Kissing leads to penetration? Penetration spreads a virus? A virus from a *dildo*? Where to begin with such outrageous thoughts?

You have seen me use the word "sign" throughout this piece, when you might have guessed "word" would be the word to use. But a sign consists of two parts: what we think of as a word ("lesbian" or "HIV," let's say) and the concept that goes with it; the word is called a signifier, the concept's called a signified; together, they're a sign. Let me simply dramatize the problem with words by sticking with "word" as the word you know. As you may have heard, a word is not itself. It cannot be one. Yes, on the page it looks singular and nicely contained: a grouping of letters accepted as a word. (We can see its form.) But to be grasped by a reader who reads it, it must quickly spawn and become a different word or group of different words that the reader uses to define the word s/he's read. In fact, the word births in us, with us, and through us, as we take it in: courtesy of us, it's allowed to *breed an intimate estrangement of itself* in the form of denotation (its socially-agreed-upon definition, contained in words that are not the word), connotations (meanings in addition to its primary meaning, held by words that are not the denotation), cultural myths that may stick to the word (as they've stuck to "lesbian" and "HIV"), along with feelings and memories the reader may attach to the word. That's a bunch of words-that-are-not-the-word that we supply when our eyes touch a word, take in one word, one solitary word, as we read it on a page. We supply these words (from prior penetrations!) from our brains and bodies, but it, the word-dildo, "stimulates" them.

We are dildoed by the word, in the sense that the word, as an object outside us, of sensuous form, must come inside us to be a word to us and to stimulate meanings (made of words-not-the-word). And though we consent to be dildoed by an author's sequencing of words — all laid out like a line of dildos — and though we're active bottoms as we take them in (even through a finger, for someone reading Braille), we are consenting to what we can't control, to a kind of transport we cannot predict.

Like one being barebacked, we consent to surface, unprotected from this surface, that starts at our surface, never knowing how a surface coming in us will breed — or die or decay. Indeed, the words bred by an author's word-dildo, never mind the copy of the word that *is* the dildo, may over time die in your body or decay. Or displace other words, causing their death or slow erosion. Even words you desperately, consciously seek to hold may not remain — or may lie dormant in ways you can't perceive (a specialty of HIV, we know).

Now let me emphasize four key points more quickly than I'd like: 1) the reader "kisses" a surface as s/he's reading; 2) we don't bugger authors, they quite impersonally dildo us; 3) reading shares a feature of barebacking that barebacking porn tries to solve; 4) reading can leave a tumescence as its trace.

Kissing is my most metaphorical claim.[iii] Who kisses with her eyes? Surely many lovers but also many readers. I say the reader kisses the word that penetrates him — that he invaginates — because I need a term for how the eye caresses, lightly or intently, the words it encounters through the reading process. A light encounter, as can happen when we're reading certain texts or parts of texts, may be like a brush of the lips in a breezy, pro-forma greeting. It's done, it's gone, it's largely instrumental. Just enough contact to get the word in. Or, perhaps, it doesn't get in. (Some words don't.)

But a more intent encounter often happens when we love a word or sequence of words, due to their "feel" — their rhythm or pulse — or mental stimulations. I call this kissing, because the uniqueness of a word-dildo, its particular feel as a surface at our surface, makes us want to linger over its exquisite properties, whether they "take us somewhere" as they enter us (as kissing can lead us down the path toward orgasm) or they are just something to caress, contact, and revisit (as kissing can take us nowhere beyond a surface we enjoy). Either way, we notice, the word like a dildo keeps its form. You could say it's mass-produced. It can be used over and over and does not belong either to the penetrator or the penetree. Moreover, it's detachable from the body wielding it. It is not its author's flesh, though it touches ours.

Can we say we're kissing the author when we're reading her? Do we bugger authors? You may consider these queries ridiculous. Over the top. But no less famous a writer than French philosopher and theorist Gilles Deleuze has written (offhandedly?) of "see[ing] the history of philosophy as a sort of buggery or (it comes to the same thing) immaculate conception." "I would imagine myself," writes Deleuze, "as taking an author from behind and giving him a child that would be his own offspring, yet monstrous." In a sense, of course, the author's words in us become a monstrous offspring: a viral growth of meanings — which might lead to a beautiful transport, we should realize. So, indeed, something is birthed. And if we wrote it down and somehow, by chance, got the author to read *our* words on the page (as a critic might succeed in doing), then we might actually penetrate him. But generally we don't.

Our sole contact with the author's body — and thus with her intent — lies in the words laid down on the page, in their certain sequence. No small thing. That is what we kiss. Dildos left by authors who were living and breathing when they left them — and their selection and arrangement reign supreme — but who may be dead and are very likely absent by the time we're kissing their words and getting pierced by them. And authors can't control their dildos' effects, never precisely and sometimes not at all, though these dildos affect quite profoundly what denotations get aroused and bred in us. (Are these fairly rational since culturally shared? Is the denotation a significant place for meanings-held-in-common with authors, other readers? Are denotations, and also connotations, what make us feel we can *argue* our points? And, indeed, we can argue, though seduction and counter-penetration are perhaps more apt descriptions for the interpretive readings we create. These are actions, still, we perform on fellow readers — more precisely, *our* readers — or consenting listeners.) In any case, connotations, cultural myths, and feelings that words conjure in us can vary strikingly from reader to reader, as the author wonderfully contaminates established words through us. However impersonal, these contacts are intimate and "come" from authors to us as a surface that will get inside us.

Of course, the getting-in-us and breeding-once-inside-us are what we cannot *see*. What a remarkable invisibility the breeding of words by the word-dildo turns out to be. Barebacking porn frets about and plans around such invisibilities. How can a viewer of porn observe a sero-conversion taking place? She can't. No one can. So Tim Dean has a fascinating chapter, "Representing Raw Sex," that discusses various imperfect methods for implying the effects that a camera cannot show (involving various maneuvers with ejaculate — and with subtitles, funnily enough). If you think of reading, a camera couldn't capture even readers' "kissing" (though it could show them looking intently at words on a page). Nor could it catch the dildo-action of a word getting into a reader's body. We can't even witness the scene of penetration common porn can show (!), never mind the stimulations of meanings, concepts, and ideas inside us. These are *mystic* materialities. We know that they are there, know they are material, but what they "are" exactly, or how they unfold, we cannot perceive. The only thing we see is what we have in common. A surface we can kiss, all of us can kiss. A word which is not one.

A word which is many words — has to be many to be a word to us — may become tumescent over time as we use it. Readers encounter words they've heard, spoken, and read many times over, making for accretions around certain terms for certain readers over time. Certain words are "swollen with significance," we say. This swollenness may happen when material experiences attach to a word and weirdly swell it for us. Therefore, what we put inside each other — even what we put in our mouths, strange to say — may affect down the line how we read a certain word.

I end with tumescence.

PENETRATING MOUTHS AND MINDS: TUMESCENT IDEAS

How are other material experiences, outside of reading but impinging on reading because they swell ideas, part of the dynamics of "lesbian" barebacking? Why would I call us ecstatic ascetics, punctured by aesthetics?[iv]

Recently, I found myself, with my undergraduates, wanting to make trouble for the word "redemption," and so, in my course, I was sliding *Pulp Fiction* onto the back of *Babette's Feast* when I found in the latter a remarkable scene of mystic materialism; surface ingestion; penetrating signifiers. This film focuses on three women: practically twinned female forms in burlap coats on the coast of the sea, who are named for Protestant revolutionaries, and a French servant who gets between their lips (women loving women, in some broad sense, women Adrienne Rich would put on "the lesbian continuum," given their lifestyle). The spare beauty of the images is such that the scoured gray of the sky makes luscious something like milk being poured in a pail. (Take that, ingestors!) The drama takes a turn when their servant, Babette, having won a lottery, asks to make the sisters and the members of their sect "a real French dinner." It's a new idea.

The Puritan sisters start to fear as the goods arrive. At night they dream of tortoise heads and spilled red wine — as if the phrase "real French dinner" and what they think it means (sinful, scary pleasures, at the very least) is at work inside them. Thus, when they warn their fellow Christians "we have exposed ourselves to [...] evil powers," they all make a pact as a way to proceed: "We shall not say a word about either food or drink; it will be as if we never have had the sense of taste." But here's what happens: a general who used to belong to their sect, who has traveled the world, attends the dinner with them and — not in on the pact of silence — exclaims his astonishment over each course, names each item they are ingesting. In fact, we as viewers watch the scene unfold from the visually engrossing actions that make the *cailles en sarcophage* (quail in sarcophagus) to the shimmering of the table, to the food itself, to the believers flush with pleasures of extraordinary wine and cuisine. And though the scene begins with the believers' "Hallelujah" and ends on the note of this very same word — as if they have simply kept their pact — the viewer is struck that between Hallelujahs sits a French dinner the believers learn to eat, block with their speech, but let in with their guts and, of course, with their minds, such that the material food they quite materially digest is set loose in some fashion around their words, so that the last Hallelujah could mean, for all we know, "mind-blowing caviar."

Here's a forceful instance of repeatable words that keep their form but tumesce over time, getting fat inside us. That is, it's a parable of what we who work in words and ideas may not see or perceive yet accomplish. What we provide between two instances of the same word — between the words "lesbian" and "lesbian," "sacrifice" and "sacrifice," "HIV" and "HIV" — are material experiences. When I teach, how I teach, when I talk, how I talk, I seek to set loose a sumptuousness surrounding words that forever changes them. This is what I like to think I have done to my students' religious words: set loose lyrical, pornological images from our reading Jean Genet, which they enjoy, around the words "pietà" or "angel" or "sacrifice."

We need not be depressed, then, as we often understandably are, to hear our students or the general culture keep talking in the same old terms. We need to believe precisely in the materiality of words. We need to believe in making words attractive (and/or newly fat) by the sensations we pack around them, in our classrooms, our interactions, our reading-in-common, and in the texture and rhythm of our words. We need to see that our words get into bodies, which may in turn breed new feelings and meanings around and for a term. Haven't fabulous femmes, for example, intervened between your former use of "woman" and your speaking the word "woman" now? (Or is that just me?)

So goes the beauty of "lesbian" barebacking. It is your beauty if you are a barebacker, which of course you are, since you are a reader, a reader reading this. You routinely kiss, indeed you bottom, your way to a reading. Then, if you share it, *it* pierces someone, via *your* dildos, and may seduce or infect their thinking, without controlling it, and plump the meanings that get attached to words and groups of words and plots-made-of-words …

Fight it though you might — close your lips to it — the signifier "lesbian" is what I've made you kiss. It is now a stranger I have made your lover, since the word "lesbian," I have suggested, stands for how words are a bold, estranging force, breeding and birthing meanings inside us. Our contact, yours and mine, does remain immaculate, for our bodies touch each other only through the dildo. But I'd like to think that, surely for a time, when you contemplate the words or ideas surrounding "reading" or "lesbian" or "kissing," you will think liquidly but no less precisely with my words inside you. Whichever words remain. Whatever dildos spread. ⫽

ENDNOTES

i. I speak of barebacking "circa '09" as it appears in Tim Dean's book. As some readers undoubtedly know, the world of barebacking is now changing, due to the drug Truvada for PrEP (pre-exposure prophylaxis), which is gaining traction among gay men, though with controversy. Will its users use the pill consistently, as it must be used so as to lower risk? Will the pill "encourage" "risky behavior"? Will it in any way affect those men who *seek* to catch the virus? For further reading, see "What Is Safe Sex? The Raw and Uncomfortable Truth About Truvada," Rich Juzwiak, http://gawker.com/what-is-safe-sex-the-raw-and-uncomfortable-truth-about-1535583252, filed last March 2014, where Tim Dean weighs in on these developments; see also "Why Is No One on the First Treatment to Prevent H.I.V.?" Christopher Glazek, *The New Yorker*, September 30, 2013. Look for Christopher Roebuck's research on these issues soon to appear.

ii. Marc Spindelman, "Sexual Freedom's Shadows," *Yale Journal of Law and Feminism*, Volume 23, No. 1, 2011, 235.

iii. For readers who would like to see my extension of this idea of reading-as-kissing, see Kathryn Bond Stockton, "Surfacing (in the Heat of Reading): Is It Like Kissing or Some Other Sex Act?" *J19*, Volume 3, Spring 2015.

iv. This section draws on and reframes materials published in my essay "Rhythm" in *Queer Times, Queer Becomings*, ed. E.L. McCallum and Mikko Tuhkanen (Albany, New York: SUNY Press, 2011), 345–48.

On the Road to Sri Bhuvaneshwari

ROBIN COSTE LEWIS

Not much larger than a Volkswagen. Smiling
        on the dashboard: Gurumukh. Marigolds
                so mild we can chew. What we call *mountain*
                        they say *foothill*. A whole vibrant green

valley of terraced balconies, rectangular
        rice farms carved into every façade
                for seven centuries. Now and then
                        a clay road washed out by rain. We wait.

Barefoot men in madras dhotis, bodies
        large only as necessity, hoist twice that in boulders
                back up the mountain, back to that place
                        where the road had been.

Monsoon. Uttar Pradesh. Twenty-eight days of rain.
        At dinner, someone says, During
                the nineteenth century, all this water
                        caused the British to go

mad. They constantly committed suicide.
        Later, someone else
                points out their Victorian cemetery.
                        I smile — a little.

That morning, seven langurs the size of six
        year olds, gray and brown, white and beige, tall tails
                curling, jumped up and down, shucked
                        and jived on top of my cold tin roof.

Somehow, I am still alive.
        I know it is wrong
                to think of a decade as lost.
                        The more I recover, the more I go

blind. Squat
        naked beside a steaming bucket.
                Hold a small cloth.
                        In Trinidad, one says *clot*.

The *h* is quiet.
        A wafer of breath — just
                like here. There's no telling
                        what languishes inside the body.

Not mist, but a whole cloud
        passes into one window,
                then two hours later,
                        out the other.

The American college students try out
        their kindergarten Hindi: *ha-pee-tal*,
                ha-pee-tal. Lips finger the sign's script,
                        then the United States break

open their mouths
        into sad smiles when they realize
                it's not Hindi, but English
                        written in Devanagari: *hospital*.

For the whole day we drive
        along miles of wet, slithering clay
                to find a temple at the top of a *mountain*
                        where Shiva is said to have once dropped

a piece of Parvati.
        Every mountaintop made holy
                by the falling charred body part
                        of the Goddess. An elbow fell

here; here
        fell Her toe; an ankle — black
                and burnt — Her knee. The road is wet and dark
                        red, and keeps spinning.

I sit behind the driver, admiring
        his cinnamon fingers, his coiffed white beard,
                his pale pink turban wrapped so handsomely.
                        Why did it take all that?

I mean, why did She have to jump
        into the celestial fire
                to prove Her purity?
                        Shiva's cool — poisonous, blue,

a shimmering galaxy —
but when it came to His Old Lady,
man, He fucked up!
Why couldn't He just believe Her?

I joke with the driver. We laugh.
Gurumukh smiles back. But then I think, perhaps
embodiment is so bewildering, even God grows
wracked with doubt.

For a certain amount
of rupees, the temple's hired a man
to announce to tourists … …*During the medieval period*
virgins were sacrificed here.

His capitalist glance mirrors our Orientalist tans.
You're lying, I say. *Save it*
for somebody pale. He smiles, passes
me a bidi. I'm bleeding, but lie

so I can go inside
and see that burnt, charred
piece of the Goddess that fell off
right here.

We climb up another one hundred
and eight stairs. At the top, I try
not to listen to anyone.
An entire Himalayan valley. Chiseled.

Every mountain — peak to base —
a living terraced verdant staircase
for the Goddess to walk down:
Sri Bhuvaneshwari.

ii.

At night, our caravan winds back
over gravel and clay. Ten headlamps
grope the mountain walls
of the green-black valley. The road

is only as wide as one small car. Hours of dog
elbows, switchbacks, half roads.

Slowly after a turn, the driver takes his foot
off the gas, downshifts, coasts.

Black.   Warm.   Breath.   Snorting.
Our car rubs against one biting grass off the face
of a cliff. Then another, taller
than our car. Then hundreds

block the road. Thick cylindrical horns scrape
the driver's window; eyes so white, black
pupils gleam, peering into our cab, grunting
and drooling onto the window.

Now the whole car, surrounded. Warm black bodies
covered in fur. Near their dusty hooves, children
sit on the ground, nested in laps, quiet and smiling.
Everyone embroidered with color:

silvers, metallic ochres, kohls, golds, reds, bold
blacks, all of it — and a green so green
I realize it's a hue
I have never seen.

A whole nomadic clan, traveling
with hundreds of water buffalo. At least
sixty human beings. There are so many
buffalo, our cars cannot move. And they can't move

the herd because a few feet ahead
a She-Buffalo is giving birth.
We get out.
And wait.

Out of habit, the students pull out their American sympathy,
but then the driver says all the women sitting there
on the ground, dusty, with children in their laps, dangling
their ankles over the mountain, adorned — all —

wear enough gold, own enough
buffalo to buy your whole house — cash.
The night holds. Life is giving birth
in the middle of a warm dark road.

Everyone in our party waits, smiling and gesturing
    with the whole clan, surrounded by snoring
        black bodies taller than our chins. We squat
           beside their lanterns, stand inside our headlight.

The driver, who grew up in this valley,
    speaks two dialects, four national languages, plus English,
        cannot understand a single word anyone says.
           Solid gold bangles, thick as bagels;

diamonds so large and rough they look
    like large cubes of clear glass. The women stare through
        their bright syllables. Then one lifts her hand, points
           at one of us — says something — and they all laugh.

iii.

The calf is born dead. A folded and wet black nothing.
    It falls out of its mother — still — onto the ground.
        We watch it in the headlamps. Empty fur sack.
        A broken umbrella made of blood and bone.

The mother tries to run. Several men hold her, throw
    broad coils of rope around her hooves. Two men, barefoot
        in dhotis, grab her on each side by her horns. And wait.
        They wait through her heaving. They sing

to her, they coo. Men who are midwives. Through
    four translations, they say it is her first time.
        She must turn around and see
           what has happened to her, or she will go mad.

We wait with the whole tribe, wait with the whole night, wait
    for her to stop bucking. Her hip bones
        are as tall as my eyes. Her neck is a massive drum.
        They do not force her, but they will not let her run.

She is pinned to the mountain, her black flat tail points down
    toward her dead newborn. There are four hands
        on her wide horns; four more hold the ropes
        that surround her haunches.

Finally, after half an hour
     of bucking and grunting, she drops her eyes
         and gives. She lowers her face into it — into the black
            slick dead thing folded on the ground —

and sniffs. Nudges the body. Snorts.
     Then they let her go. She runs off, back
         into the snoring herd.
            Disappears.

iv.

One day, ten years later — one fine, odd day — suddenly
     I will remember all of this. That night, that dark
         narrow road will come back. Like a small sleepy child, it will sit
            gently down inside my lap, and look up into me.

Kohl and camphor around all the babies' eyes
     to keep evil away; that exquisite smell of men
         and sweat and dust; the unanticipated calm
            of standing within

an enormous herd of sleeping water buffalo, listening.
     To spend your entire life — out of doors — walking the world
         with your whole family and neighborhood. To stay
            together, to leave together. *What a blessing*, I think,

and then, *What a curse!*
     My newborn is asleep in a red wagon
         that says *Radio Flyer.* I have packed
            a large suitcase and one box.

The World wants to know
     what I am made of. I am trying
        to find a way
          to answer Her.

I place our things by the door. And wait.
     Standing. Eyes closed. Looking. I want to
         remember the carved angels flying over the tall bay
            windows; the front door's twelve perfect squares

of beveled glass; the cloud-high ceilings;
          the baby's stuffed monkey; the tribal rugs; and the photograph
                    of our tent in the desert that one soundless morning, on the floor
                              of a canyon in Jordan. All in boxes now.

The lights are on. The house
          is empty. Night comes.
                    I smell the giant magnolia blossoms
                              opening.

Once, I thought I was a person with a body,
          the body of something peering
                    out, enchanted
                              and tossed.

The baby wakes. He is almost four
          weeks old. I give him a piece
                    of my body. He fingers my necklace
                              strung with green glass beads.

I tie him onto my back and think about the brazen
          dahlias, nursed from seeds, staging a magenta riot now,
                    next to the rusty Victorian daybed, where he was conceived,
                              beneath the happy

banana tree out on the back balcony.
          My father's gold earrings are welded into my ears.
                    My mother's diamonds are folded
                              into a handkerchief inside my pocket.

And then, as if
          it is the most natural thing to do, I walk
                    toward the stairwell, and give
                              the World my answer.

All the way down the staircase, my hand palms
          the mahogany rail, and I think, Once
                    this beam of wood stood high
                              inside a great dark forest.

v.

Thick coat. Black fur. Two russet horns
        twisted to stone. One night
                I was stuck on a narrow road,
                        panting.

I was pregnant.
        I was dead.
                I was a fetus.
                        I was just born
(Most days
        I don't know what I am).
                I am a photograph
                        of a saint, smiling.

For years, my whole body ran
        away from me. When I flew — charred —
                through the air, my ankles and toes fell off
                        onto the peaks of impassable mountains.

I have to go back
        to that wet black thing
                dead in the road. I have to turn around.
                        I must put my face in it.

It is my first time.
        I would not have it any other way.
                I am a valley of repeating
                        verdant balconies. ◢

ANDREA BOWERS

I VALUE AN ARTIST'S voice over the aesthetics of an artwork. Aesthetics should be in service of the content of a work of art, not its subject. I want to make all the necessary information available to the viewer — art can compel its viewers to deeper contemplation when its meaning is clearly readable. I deplore the belief that art should privilege the autographical subjectivity of its maker and turn information into decoration. Nor do I relate to the attempt to create an "open-endedness" in order to leave interpretation up to the viewer.

I make work about activists who dedicate their lives to social justice through direct action and protest. I record the actions of those who believe in the right to self-determination, self-government, and freedom. As an artist and as a feminist, I aim to play a role in building a culture free of sexism, misogyny, and male-centeredness. I use my practice as a tool for creating alternatives to heteronormative thinking and for the obliteration of racism and xenophobia. This means opening borders, tearing down fences, free healthcare, free education, and a living wage; ending the unjust disparity of wealth, the prison industrial complex, violence against women (both cis and trans), and clamoring for climate justice. I believe artists should embed themselves in a meaningful way in communities of resistance and allow these communities to be inspirational and collaborative: meaningful conversation, political organizing, teaching, and civil disobedience are also mediums of art. A political art practice need not be void of emotion or beauty as long as it is in service of liberation. ✍

SISTERS BE STRONG, 2013
MARKER ON FOUND CARDBOARD
APPROXIMATELY 4' 6" X 8' 6"
COURTESY OF THE ARTIST AND KAUFMANN REPETTO, MILAN

FIGHT FOR $15 MARCH (DECEMBER 4, 2014), 2015
GRAPHITE ON PAPER, 15 X 22"
COURTESY OF THE ARTIST AND SUSANNE VIELMETTER LOS ANGELES PROJECTS
PHOTO: ROBERT WEDEMEYER

BROWN BERET YOUNG WOMAN WITH BULLETS (LA RAZA, VOL. III, NO. 9, NOVEMBER 1969, L.A. PG. 4), 2015
GRAPHITE ON PAPER, 30 X 22.25"
COURTESY OF THE ARTIST AND KAUFMANN REPETTO, MILANO
PHOTO: ANDREA ROSSETTI

TOP TO BOTTOM:
*ANONYMOUS MOTHER AND CHILD
(STEUBENVILLE RAPE CASE TRIAL,
STEUBENVILLE, OH, MARCH, 14, 2013)*, 2015
GRAPHITE ON PAPER
15 X 22.25"
COURTESY OF THE ARTIST AND SUSANNE
VIELMETTER LOS ANGELES PROJECTS
PHOTO: ROBERT WEDEMEYER

*ANONYMOUS WOMAN (STEUBENVILLE RAPE
CASE TRIAL, STEUBENVILLE, OH, MARCH 14,
2013)*, 2015
GRAPHITE ON PAPER
15 X 22.25"
COURTESY OF THE ARTIST AND SUSANNE
VIELMETTER LOS ANGELES PROJECTS
PHOTO: JEFF MCLANE

*#JUSTICEFORJANEDOE, ANONYMOUS
WOMEN PROTESTORS, STEUBENVILLE RAPE
CASE, MARCH 13 – 17, 2013)*, 2014
GRAPHITE ON PAPER
30 X 22.5"
COURTESY OF THE ARTIST AND SUSANNE
VIELMETTER LOS ANGELES PROJECTS
PHOTO: ROBERT WEDEMEYER

FROM DC TO STEUBENVILLE (STEUBENVILLE RAPE CASE TRIAL, STEUBENVILLE, OH, MARCH 14, 2013), 2015
GRAPHITE ON PAPER
15 X 22.25"
COURTESY OF THE ARTIST AND SUSANNE VIELMETTER LOS ANGELES PROJECTS
PHOTO: JEFF MCLANE

ONE BIG UNION, 2012
MARKER ON FOUND CARDBOARD, 157 x 105"
COURTESY OF THE ARTIST AND SUSANNE VIELMETTER LOS ANGELES PROJECTS. PHOTO: ROBERT WEDEMEYER

ONEILL - TRIUMPH OF LABOR (TITLE TO BE CONFIRMED), 2015
ARCHIVAL MARKER ON CARDBOARD, 122.5 X 98.5"
COURTESY OF THE ARTIST AND SUSANNE VIELMETTER LOS ANGELES PROJECTS. PHOTO: JEFF MCLANE

TRANS LIBERATION: BEAUTY IS IN THE STREET I (JOHANNA SAAVEDRA). 2015.
COURTESY OF THE ARTIST AND ANDREW KREPS GALLERY, NY

TRANS LIBERATION: NI UNA MAS, NOT ONE MORE (JENNICET GUTIERREZ). 2015.
COURTESY OF THE ARTIST AND ANDREW KREPS GALLERY, NY

TRANS LIBERATION: VISIBILITY IS NOT ENOUGH I (CECE MCDONALD). 2015.
COURTESY OF THE ARTIST AND ANDREW KREPS GALLERY, NY

A GARLAND FOR MAY DAY (ILLUSTRATION BY WALTER CRANE), 2012
MARKER ON FOUND CARDBOARD, 156 x 140"
COURTESY OF THE ARTIST AND SUSANNE VIELMETTER LOS ANGELES PROJECTS
PHOTO: ROBERT WEDEMEYER

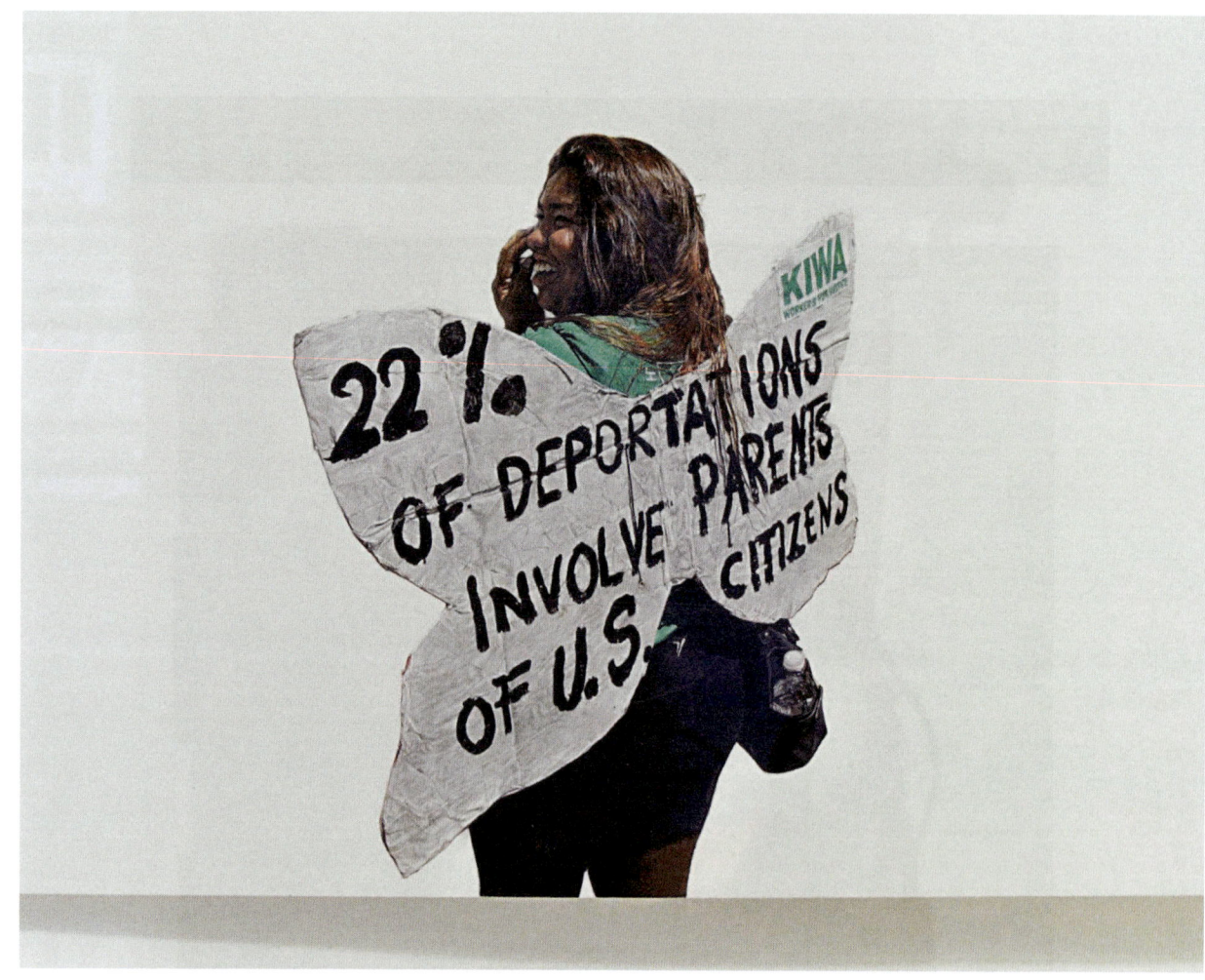

22% OF DEPORTATIONS INVOLVE PARENTS OF U.S. CITIZENS
(IMMIGRANT JUSTICE ACTIVIST, MAY DAY 2014, LOS ANGELES), 2014
COLORED PENCIL ON PAPER, 23.23 x 15.94"
COURTESY OF THE ARTIST, KAUFMANN REPETTO, MILANO,
WITH THE SUPPORT OF ESPACE CULTUREL LOUIS VUITTON
PHOTO: SEBASTIANO PELLION DI PERSANO

R: *FOR MY TRANSGENDER SISTERS (MAY DAY MARCH, LOS ANGELES, 2012)*, 2012
COLORED PENCIL ON PAPER, 30 x 22"
COURTESY OF THE ARTIST AND SUSANNE VIELMETTER LOS ANGELES PROJECTS
PHOTO: ROBERT WEDEMEYER

SUPPORT THE DREAM (PASS THE DREAM ACT), 2013
COLORED PENCIL ON PAPER, 30 x 22"
COURTESY OF THE ARTIST AND KAUFMANN REPETTO, MILAN

L: LEGALIZE MY MAN (MAY DAY MARCH, LOS ANGELES, 2012), 2012
COLORED PENCIL ON PAPER, 30 x 22"
COURTESY OF THE ARTIST AND SUSANNE VIELMETTER LOS ANGELES PROJECTS
PHOTO: ROBERT WEDEMEYER

CHARLES GAINES
NUMBERS AND TREES II, #6 HAFIR, 1987
ACRYLIC SHEET, ACRYLIC PAINT, INK AND MASONITE; 48 X 39 1/2"
COURTESY OF THE ARTIST SUSANNE VIELMETTER LOS ANGELES PROJECTS; PHOTO: STEVEN PROBERT

THE FUNCTION OF CRITICISM AT THE PRESENT TIME

VIRGINIA JACKSON

LAUREN BERLANT is a critic's critic, a feminist's feminist, and a thinker's friend. This is most simply true because of the number, depth, and influence of her abundant authored and co-authored and edited and co-edited books, her ever more numerous articles, essays, interviews, dialogues and monologues, and especially her proliferating collaborations; she always seems to be writing yet another book with yet another interesting someone else. Lots of people think with and because of Lauren Berlant. But academic "productivity" (that ubiquitous and ugly word, itself a symptom of the corporate manufacture of a crisis in the humanities) isn't the most important reason that my first proposition — that Berlant is a critic's critic — is just true. The reason that Lauren Berlant occupies this moment in critical theory so capaciously is that what she really always thinks about is genre.

Once upon a time, or so the story goes, the genre system was hierarchical and taxonomic (though not so fixed that at least as early as Aristotle's *Poetics* it wasn't open to debate), with "tragedies" clearly separated from "comedies," for example. Later, in modernity (the novel is usually considered both the origin and result of this shift), genres became modes of recognition — complex forms instantiated in popular discourse, relying on what we could or would recognize *collectively, in common* — and so subject to historical change and cultural negotiation. Once genres became historical, the story continues, it then became the critic's job to manage and translate those emerging forms of recognition for the benefit of readers who experienced them without knowing exactly what it was they were seeing and feeling.

Genre seems like an old-fashioned, belletristic frame to impose on Berlant's political, cultural, and affective range. I may be wrong, but I'm betting that if I asked you to think of a queer theorist, Berlant is one of the first critics you would name, and if I asked you to think of a theorist of public culture or affect or performativity or media publics or marginal aesthetics or crisis, Berlant would be one of the first critics you would name, but if I asked you to think of a genre theorist, Berlant would not be the first critic to come to mind. No one would accuse Lauren Berlant of being a purely literary critic.

Yet like Eve Sedgwick or Paul de Man or Edward Said — the game-changing critical theorists of the end of the last century, to which Berlant's work bears comparison — Berlant is a laureate of genre, which is to say that Berlant pays attention to what critical theory is made of. If modern literary criticism invented the concept of genre in order to invent itself (and I think it did), then Berlant thinks about genre in order to think about the function of criticism at the present time.

My allusion to Matthew Arnold is not as funny as it may seem, despite the fact that Arnold is usually considered the standard bearer of a 19th-century Victorian cultural conservatism completely antithetical to Berlant's 21st-century queer radicalism. Arnold cultivated a disinterested position of refined critical appreciation and characterized middlebrow taste as "Philistine"; Berlant delights in mass culture and in its passionately interested investments. Yet if the function of criticism for Arnold was normative, it was also utopian, since "the true life of literature" was for him "the promised land, towards which criticism can only beckon." Arnold's critic is also always an outsider: "That promised land it will not be ours to enter, and we shall die in the wilderness: but to have desired to enter it, to have saluted it from afar, is already, perhaps, the best distinction among contemporaries."

For Berlant, too, the function of criticism is to invite us into the fiction of a promised land, but unlike Arnold, she does not foreclose entrance to that promise by insisting on its fictitiousness. After all, what forms of desire are not fictive? How could we get out of bed in the morning without taking our fictions with us? If genre is normative in the sense that it invites you into a fantasy that (once you realize that it is a fantasy) returns you to or keeps you in your place (pathetically happy in your disappointment), then the thing that makes Berlant our Arnold in drag, the current diva performer of the function of criticism at the present time, is that she keeps trying to think past the contemporary consensus that genres themselves are normative because they are communally held forms of recognition.

Berlant wants that recognition to mean that genres can become the vehicles of social change, or at least of degrees of adjustment. She can skate the outlines of received genres with more precision than any of us, but she also wants to make those boundaries turn out toward a utopian horizon where the barriers between us may not exactly fall but will be illuminated as shared in what Berlant likes to call "the history of the present." As she said recently in an interview on the "Society and Space" blog (as an old friend of mine once said, Berlant "has a lot of language," so the interview is a good genre for her, and the blogosphere a good generic medium, since so much of the language she has so much of can overflow and circulate there), "it's never about shaming people's objects, it's always about creating better and better objects. It's always about creating better worlds, making it possible for us to think in more and different kinds of ways about how we relationally can move through life." If for Arnold the function of criticism at the present time was to help us agree to be mutually and soberly bummed out, to move through life in a shared state of exile from literary scenes of fulfillment, distinguished only by our cultivated taste for more such disappointments, for Berlant the function of criticism at the present time is to create better worlds, worlds in which genres are not settled states of common disappointment and classed distinction in the experience and expression of that disappointment, but are instead signs and figures for shared world making.

"Successfully accomplished genre is a utopian performance, a scene of mastery in contrast to disappointing life, with its rhythm of failed experiments," Berlant writes in *The Female Complaint: The Unfinished Business of Sentimentality in American Culture* (2008). The trick that Berlant recommends is to move through life *as if* it were the utopian performance of genre. We're not to buy the promised land fantasy, but we're not to give up on it either, not to mistake the sign of belonging that is not world making for the sign that might be. The recognition of that sign is not a mark of distinction or taste, as Arnold would have had it, but itself constitutes what Berlant calls "an intimate public sphere."

The contradiction inherent in the space between those two adjectives is not ironic, unless irony is a word for the way we live our lives (and I don't think that Berlant thinks that it is or can be, which is what separates her from the critics of the end of the last century and is another way Berlant opens a new direction for the function of criticism at the present time). What "intimate public" holds in phrase is the way in which genres address us, hail us, and then (and this is the important turn) the way in which we enter that scene of address, the ways in which we live there, so that the given little by little becomes what is made. The personal is the generic, but the generic is also personal. The sympathetic embrace and the unrelenting analysis of the genericization of the personal is Berlant's signature double move, capacities that Arnold granted to criticism but that his criticism could not compass, perhaps because they turn out to be the special talents of critics who think and feel — intimately, publicly — as women.

I focus here on *The Female Complaint* not because it is Berlant's most recent book (it is not) or her best book (though it may be) but because in it she has so much to say about what makes women such agile practitioners of criticism at the present time. The book maps the intimate twists and turns by means of which genre as a mode of cultural creation and interpretation becomes indistinguishable from genre as a shaping force in lived experience. Since "femininity is a genre with deep affinities to the genres associated with femininity," it makes sense that for Berlant, women would be skilled in the genres (both literary and lived) of romance and (particularly heteronormative) sentiment — writing them, reading them, and living them. But it turns out that even though *The Female Complaint* is mostly about those especially feminine genres, women have a knack for genre *theory* as well — for what Arnold would have called criticism — because genre is the stuff of which women, like criticism, are made.

The preface to *The Female Complaint* is a bravura performance of that knack. Here are its first two paragraphs:

> Previous versions of this preface narrated how emotionally thorny it was to write this book. I wrote of myself and of women in my particular family — from Lena and Sadie to Mara and Cindy — who entered femaleness at different historical moments and yet whose styles of being in femininity have contained uncanny similarities. As you can imagine, such resonances raised intensities of attachment, love, protectiveness, gratitude, disappointment, despair, anger, and resentment that created obstacles to lithesome storytelling.

> Then a friend not from the humanities asked me, "Why are you airing your personal business here? Isn't your knowledge the point?" Right, I responded — well, in the humanities we try to foreground what motivates and shapes our knowledge, and a personal story can telegraph a perspective efficiently and humanly. I wasn't happy with this somewhat canned response, although I also believe it. Yet the autobiographical isn't the personal. This nonintuitive phrase is a major presupposition of *The Female Complaint*. In the contemporary consumer public, and in the *longue durée* that I'm tracking, all sorts of narratives are read as autobiographies of collective experience. The personal is the general. Publics presume intimacy.

Within these sentences, Berlant moves from personal professional embarrassment (with its designer handbag full of unprofessional affective attachments and detachments) to a concise definition of the episteme of current work in the humanities to the limits of that episteme to the "major presupposition" of her book, which turns out to push those limits back in the direction of the personal confession she only seems to have sidelined, since "the personal is the general." The personal is not autobiographical. The personal is generic.

I'm reminded here of what Michael Warner said about Judith Butler's early work, that

> where most accounts of norms imagine an agent who acts on the basis of beliefs or desires and reflects on what ought to be done, Butler called attention to the ways we find ourselves already normatively organized as certain kinds of agents, for example by having gender in ways that must be intelligible to others.

In Berlant's work, and especially in *The Female Complaint*, we find ourselves organized as certain kinds of agents because we are organized by *genre* in ways that are already intelligible to others because genres are sites of mutual collective recognition.

These sites of recognition are what make up the genders we seem to be and have: "femininity is a genre with deep affinities to the genres associated with femininity." Berlant's working premise is more radical than Butler's. Yes, gender is performative for Berlant, but the critic's task is not to analyze that performativity itself but instead to trace the kooky outlines of the genres that make it possible.

The thing is, genre is a heartbreaker. The plaintiveness of *The Female Complaint* and the cruelty of *Cruel Optimism* (2011) both turn on the turn that genre takes when its utopian promise breaks down, when our experiments in living can't remain or become experiments in genre, since, as Berlant writes in *Cruel Optimism*, "genres provide an affective expectation of the experience of watching something unfold, whether that thing is in life or in art." If that generic expectation is too starry-eyed, genre will fold up its fragile tents: "A relation of cruel optimism exists when something you desire is actually an obstacle to your flourishing"; "Everyone knows what the female complaint is: women live for love, and love is the gift that keeps on taking."

So the trick is to adjust or loosen expectations to make and consume aesthetic frames for experience that don't set one up for such letdowns, or, in one of Berlant's apparently infinite ways of phrasing the feminized version of this trick, "women's disappointing experiences of the normal forms of personhood and intimacy do not induce rejection of them, but improvisations on *the fear of the loss of the melancholic position* that arises from stark consciousness of normalcy's apparitional solidity." (I told you, lots of language — Berlant must get tired of how often her Word program turns her writing choices red and green — but it's a good thing that she has learned to ignore even the generic censors in her software.)

One way to improvise, of course, is to give up one's dreams of freedom from constraint, including generic constraint. In *Cruel Optimism* and her recent collaborative, interactive, blogging, and essayistic work, Berlant has become increasingly interested in what she describes as "the becoming historical of the affective event and the improvisation of genre amid pervasive uncertainty. [...] The waning of genre frames different kinds of potential openings within and beyond the impasse of adjustment that constant crisis creates." One might work around the cruelty of optimism or the setup for complaint by scaling back the intensity of one's investments in genre, especially in the genres of the happy ending or the good life.

As those genres come to seem more fictitious and less attainable, the culture of crisis and precarity of most contemporary lives might have alternative possibilities. The waning of genre means that contemporary forms of recognition are up for grabs, and so the communal investments in those forms of recognition (what Berlant likes to call "fantasies of the good life") might also change. (If the mortgage for the house with the picket fence is unattainable, maybe that genre will give way to more sustainable housing; if weddings are too expensive, maybe there will be fewer disappointed and mistreated brides; queer and trans modes of adaptation in these as in other respects become models for our common survival.) Because women are made of such investments, they have a lot of practice in adjustments of scale, and in this way as well women are calibrated to the critical history of the present. We have serious skills in managing the treachery of genre.

Some of us more than others. The chapter on Dorothy Parker in *The Female Complaint* seems to me exemplary of everything I have been saying about Berlant. What Berlant writes about Parker in this chapter goes double for Berlant herself:

> Parker's [read: Berlant's] work focuses on the centrality of genre to the elusive experience of being held by the promise of the normal as ideal. Genre is her scene of *whateverness*, Giorgio Agamben's term for the condition of an ethical belonging to the social as a matter of its being such, regardless of program or content. Parker's [read: Berlant's] fidelity to the social is expressed in her commitment to genre.

I want to linger on Berlant's virtuoso reading of Parker, but first it is worth noticing that what Berlant admires in Parker and I admire in Berlant is a relation of criticism in Arnold's sense, of "the effort," as Arnold put it, "for now many years […] to see the object as in itself it really is." What I'm arguing here is this: Berlant is really a genre theorist as Berlant argued in *The Female Complaint* that Parker was really a genre theorist as Parker argued that genres are what really make sociality possible, though that possibility will kill you if you don't make yourself a theorist and tell genre like it is.

This is to say that for Parker genres were always already normatively organizing, while Berlant and I hope in different ways that this might not always or necessarily be so, at least not if we are good enough critics to imagine an alternative. If genre is Parker's scene of *whateverness*, it is not Berlant's, at least not in our contemporary affective sense of the *whatever*, since Berlant is much more of a utopian thinker than Parker was, and certainly more of a utopian thinker than I am. For Berlant, "a genre is a loose affectively-invested zone of expectations about the narrative shape a situation will take," and the effort of the critic is always to imagine a better or more interesting or more malleable or generous story: the goal of criticism is to make the stories that surround us, whether their fictions are literary or lived, *more interesting*.

But what about when the genre at stake is not narrative; what about when it is a poem that does not tell an unfolding story but that instead formalizes and enacts the intractable work of genre?

Berlant is fascinated by Parker's poetry, partially because it does not quite participate in Berlant's otherwise very narrative and therefore ongoing and unfolding understanding of how genres work. In her reading of the great "Sonnet for the End of a Sequence," Berlant points out that Parker "does not even bother to tell the story that propels us to the predictable end":

> So take my vows and scatter them to sea;
> Who swears the sweetest is no more than human.
> And say no kinder words than these of me:
> "Ever she longed for peace, but was a woman!

And thus they are, whose silly female dust
Needs little enough to clutter it and bind it,
Who meet a slanted gaze, and ever must
Go build themselves a soul to dwell behind it."

For now I am my own again, my friend!
This scar but points the whiteness of my breast;
This frenzy, like its betters, spins an end,
And now I am my own. And that is best.
Therefore, I am immeasurably grateful
To you, for proving shallow, false, and hateful.

"If the details did matter to the story of a woman," Berlant somewhat wistfully begins after citing the sonnet,

> one might talk about the poet's irony, detailing her measured assertion of immeasurable gratitude at being so beautifully and confirmingly disappointed and abandoned, and showing how intricately the sounds of the double lettered words — silly, little, cluttered, betters — resonate with the other couplings expressed in the end rhymes, distressed in the enjambments, and inverted in the end, where the poet belies her earlier demonstration of virtuosic femininity in love and in the genres of love that she can write, with emotion, and shape, into beauty, and imitate, as from an elevated tradition of witnessing, what is finally identical to her own soul's desires. It is as though Parker wants to show that she has mastered (poetic) convention rather than being mastered by it (emotionally). But the process of the poetry is to master the compliant reader until that compliance hits the female complaint. […] What Parker works here is the revelation of the process of holding on to the form and staying thereby in proximity to the norm.

The performance of the *as if* of genre fantasy is only imaginable for Berlant as a story. Since Parker "does not even bother to tell the story," Berlant makes one up, or makes up the way in which the story *would* be told if Parker were telling it, which she is not.

Instead, Parker, like Berlant, adjusts "the genres of love that she can write" to her circumstances, but that adjustment can only take the form of mastering the form of the sonnet itself, which ends (as genres always threaten to do) by biting her in the ass, or end (of a missing but known sequence of love won and lost). In Berlant's account, the maintenance of proximity to the norm exemplified by the revenge of the sonnet is essentially masochistic:

> Averse to conventionality, but relieved of singularity through it too, sometimes it is all a girl can do to show you a once beautiful shape, a failed conventional form, or an instance of tinny courage that can gesture toward the broken utopian while making you feel the optimism of having an infinite number of second chances at it.

Sometimes. But as gorgeously identified and disidentified as Berlant's reading of Parker is, even this reading may not go as far as Parker did in making the generic constitution of gender an all-or-nothing game in which there are no second chances. The sonnet is not a story; it is a sonnet, and a double-dog-dare-you sonnet at that, announcing its Italianate break between the octave and the sestet and then adding an Elizabethan couplet as a second *volta* for extra fun.

Its genre is thus already a palimpsest, and that palimpsest gets more palimpsestic when the direct address to the reader puts misogynist words in that interpellated reader's mouth and then turns (first *volta*) from us before we can spit them out. Is it our misogyny that has driven her away, or the misogyny of the guy (we assume it was a guy) who abandoned her in the first place?

Berlant is surely right that the second *volta*, the closing couplet, performs a masochistic refusal of the question, but that masochism also depends on an inherited genre: the Poetess sonnet. Barrett Browning's *Sonnets from the Portuguese* may be the best-known surviving 19th-century sequence of such poems, but in the second half of the 19th century there were hundreds if not thousands of Poetess sonnets, a tradition echoed and varied by Parker's contemporary Edna St. Vincent Millay, among many others. The second line of the sestet ("This scar but points the whiteness of my breast") is the dead giveaway, since the generic figure of the Poetess (capitalized to emphasize its generic character, and to avoid confusion with any particular woman poet) was known by the thorn that pierced the nightingale's breast in poem after poem fifty or a hundred years before Parker tried her hand at one.

In its heyday, the Poetess poem created and was the property of an intimate public sphere very much like the mass publics for melodramas and happy endings Berlant describes so vividly in *The Female Complaint*. The repeated generic outlines of the suffering woman became the vehicle for shared identifications and disidentifications of all sorts for a century before Parker's sonnet appeared. The Poetess was the figure that made the personal generic in the first place.

The Poetess sonnet itself thus maps the *longue durée* of the archive of Berlant's book, since it testifies in every line to "the unfinished business of sentimentality in American culture," business begun in earnest by the women writers of the 19th century. But the thing about such long historical arcs is that tracing them can put one out of step with one's contemporaries; like Millay, Parker invokes a genre that no longer flourished as an intimate public sphere by the middle of the 20th century. That built-in waning of genre also seems to me to speak to Berlant's point in the book (*Cruel Optimism*) that would follow *The Female Complaint* that "the waning of genre frames different kinds of potential openings within and beyond the impasse of adjustment that constant crisis creates."

Berlant thinks that Parker is demonstrating the sonnet's intransigence and that the poet played the transhistorically fixed form of the sonnet off against the female complaint in order to shock her readers into an acknowledgment of the difference between life and genre. Berlant's view is in this sense like Benjamin's understanding of Baudelaire as a poet who wrote for readers who no longer liked lyric poetry and had to be shocked into paying attention. But I think that Parker knew that the Poetess sonnet already did what Berlant thinks Parker did, and did it better a century earlier. By the time of Parker's sonnet, the figure of the Poetess had become a figure in the carpet, and the untimeliness of Parker's performance of that figure is what creates the opening through which we can see the inside and the outside of genre, the inside and outside of gender, at the same time and from a distance.

From that slightly blurry perspective, Parker would be reading the Poetess in the way that Berlant would be reading Parker and, not incidentally, in the way I have been reading Berlant. We are all dizzy dames trying to think our ways out of the genres of which we are made.

By thinking with Berlant in the language of the history of poetics in which I feel more at home than in her language of narrative form, I have hoped to demonstrate how thinking with Berlant does not mean agreeing with her. How could it? She is much too generous to want your agreement, and her generosity is inspiring.

What Lauren Berlant wants is for you to join her in trying to figure out what in the world we can do with and about the genres in which we choose or in which we are forced to live. In the last century, criticism might have dwelled on the pathos of uncertainty located in that "or," but I think that Berlant takes the function of criticism at the present time into the history of the present by not putting her emphasis on irony or pathos. Melancholia (for lost promises, lost genres, impossible worlds) may be inevitable, but thinking beyond the melancholic position can be an exhilarating if unstable enterprise.

Dorothy Parker (between drinks) wanted to do that, too, and so do I, though Berlant somehow manages more conviction (despite herself) than most of the rest of us do on a normal day that such thinking will make a difference, or maybe that the thinking is just worth doing because it is what critics (and women) do best.

Berlant makes me believe what Arnold believed, that "to have the sense of creative activity is the great happiness and the great proof of being alive, and it is not denied to criticism to have it; but then criticism must be sincere, simple, flexible, ardent, ever widening its knowledge." It would surprise Arnold to find that he had described in advance the criticism of Lauren Berlant, and it might surprise her even more to find that Arnold's dream of the good life for criticism turned out after all to have her name on it. ◢

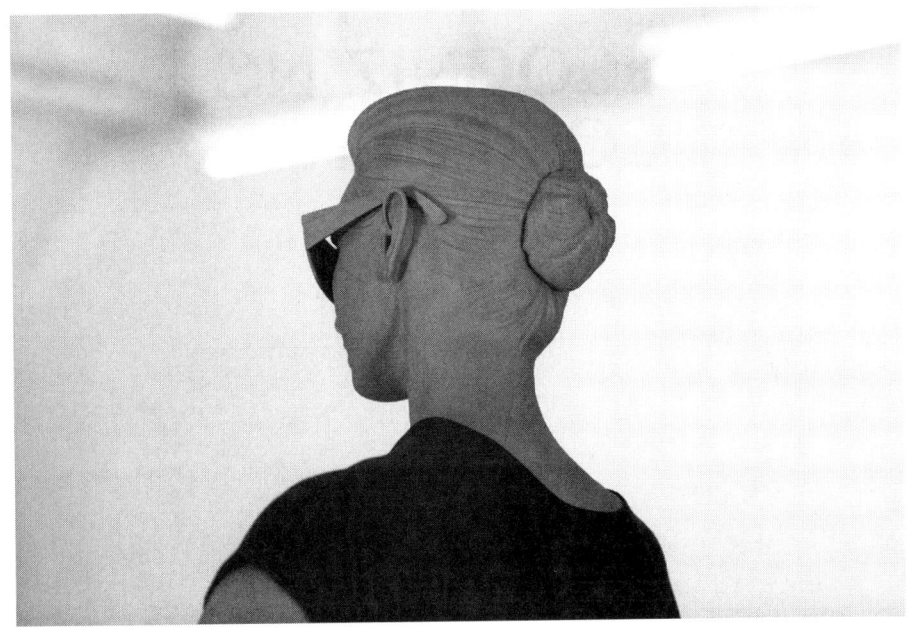

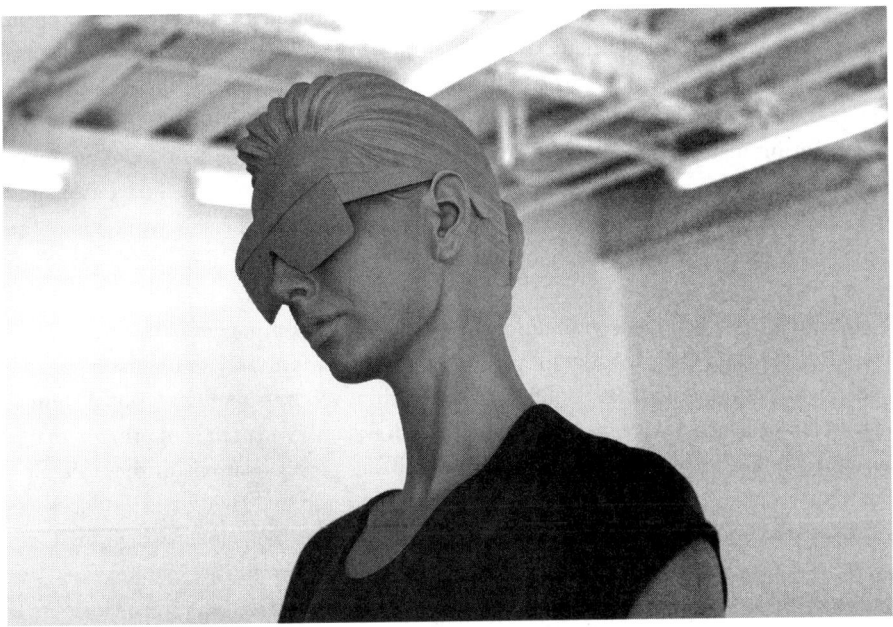

FRANK BENSON
HUMAN STATUE (JESSIE) (DETAIL), 2011
BRONZE, MARBLE; 79 1/4 X 12 1/2 X 20"
COURTESY OF THE ARTIST AND ANDREW KREPS GALLERY, NEW YORK

RECOGNIZING COMPLICITY

JOHANNA DRUCKER

T. J. CLARK begins the first long essay in *Farewell to an Idea* with a measured but keen sense of drama, reporting two major historical events while gesturing to pressing issues offstage: On October 16, 1793 (or 25 Vendémiaire Year 2), "a hastily completed painting by Jacques-Louis David, of Marat, the martyred hero of the revolution [...] was released into the public realm." At midday on that same day, "Marie-Antoinette was guillotined. Michelet tells us that her death, so long demanded by Hébert and the Paris wards (the so-called *sections*), in the event went off quietly. People's minds were on other things [...]." In an immediate engagement with the portrait of the dead Marat in his bath, we can easily forget intimately its production is bound to those "other things" — ongoing upheaval and revolutionary struggles — and yield to a reductive iconographic reading of the image through its overt references to a deposed Christ. But universalizing Marat's depiction in David's work misses the import of its identity as a modern work, situated in and formulated in response to a specific set of conditions and circumstances.

As Clark's discussion of the portrait unfolds, he brings every component of its formal construction (brushwork, degree of finish, iconography, lighting, composition, and draughtsmanship) into an intricate dialogue with the unfolding political events within which its representational strategies were conceived, and in which they were meant to signify. He draws on a wide range of primary materials and synthetic accounts to present a study of the rapidly shifting power relations in the unstable political climate. So, for instance, he quotes the four-line poem composed by David's friend Gabriel Bouquier (calling for the death to be avenged) that was pinned to Marat's bier, cites passages by Citizen (the Marquis de) Sade condemning Charlotte Corday, that "soft and timid sex," to her fate ("break this monster in pieces"), uses contemporary accounts from *L'Ami du Peuple*, and gleans insights from the vast scholarly literature covering the history of this complex period of the Revolution.

The result is a presentation of the work within the "cult of Marat" where allegiances and alliances were shifting day by day, sometimes hour by hour. The "image" (painting and idea) of Marat had to flirt with martyrdom while avoiding certain overt features of religious and secular clichés that might sidetrack viewers from the cause. The painting, in other words, cannot simply be "read" in its evident

JACQUES-LOUIS DAVID
MARAT ASSASSINATED, 1793
OIL ON CANVAS, 65 X 50 1/2"
BEQUEST JULES-DAVID CHASSAGNOL,
PARIS, 1886; ROYAL MUSEUMS OF
FINE ARTS OF BELGIUM, BRUSSELS

materiality. (Clark is anything but a formalist, in spite of the strength of his eye and sensitivity to construction.) Each element of that visual making has to be seen as integral to decisions made by David within constraints that conditioned the painting's production. The elaborate "stage managing" of its presentation was crucial to the value and the reception of the work. Politics is what the portrait of Marat is made of, Clark asserts, and to make form out of it, David created the quickly painted image to signify the realization that Marat was "a political sign to be controlled." Ultimately, Clark concludes, David's goal was to "return Marat to the people through the combination of visual codes and spectacular events within which it came to public view."

The long chapter is replete with carefully chosen evidence whose judicious use depends upon sustained research and the craft of argument. To be aware of these various materials, and understand their connection to the painting and its circumstances of first exhibition, is the essence of scholarly practice. Throughout, Clark's work is a compelling demonstration of the humanities as a field of intellectual work essential to our understanding of present and past as a never simple interpretation of the material record. Nothing in that record, including the paintings that are Clark's major concern, is self-evident. Interpretation is argument, and Clark's is deeply felt. How, he asks, are we to understand the history of modernism (aesthetic work) in the face of the overwhelming triumph of modernity (capital)? How was that history written? On what terms and by what critical method did it proceed to construct (and not merely reflect) a set of beliefs about representation and the role of painting? The answers to these questions form the framework of the book. They raise issues of method central to epistemology and politics. How do we know what we know? On what grounds do we understand the representations we make to ourselves of our beliefs, individually and collectively? In this case, how are we to understand what is being lost as modernism comes to an end, and what is at stake in coming to terms with our current condition? The humanities are disciplines, after all, and claims for the value of "the humanities" benefit from a solid foundation. Clark's work is a superb example of what constitutes the humanities at its most professionally adept and passionately significant.

Clark's method is premised on recognition of loss. He knows that once the reference frames by which we read works have completely disappeared, their meaning disappears or alters radically. These once-legible images have become obscure or are misconstrued. "Modernism," says Clark, "is our antiquity." In other words, the 19th and even 20th centuries are already so remote that their remains, their "forms of its representation [… are] now unreadable." His goal in this project (the book was first published in 1999) was not simply to create readings of works that marked shifts and change points in the longer history of modern art, but to construct an examination of the fragments and remains of a past that can no longer simply *be read* as if they are self-evident (if they ever could). "Modernism" in this context refers to a set of cultural practices, "modernity" to historical (political and economic) conditions that arise with industrialization and modern capitalism. To understand how representational activity, specifically painting, worked in and as modernism, he does not just read what is *in* these images, but reads them as expressions of beliefs, philosophical concerns with negation, visibility, anarchism, and as a semiotics through which to decry the monstrousness of the modern world.

The elegiac tone of Clark's book is signaled in its title, *Farewell to an Idea*. The work was marked by the moments of its conception, when certain long-held beliefs could no longer be sustained. Clark started thinking about these essays just as the Berlin Wall fell. The momentousness of this event, celebrated as an end to the oppressions of the Cold War, coincided with a common perception that the project of socialism was at an end. Many theorists and historians of modernism had believed aesthetics and politics were bound together. But with the political changes, the hope that a mature form of socialism could assert a check, even a constraint, on unchecked capitalism was up for question. If socialism and modernism were dying at the same moment, he asked, did that mean that their existence and life spans had been intertwined, mutually determined? The "social project" and the representational explorations were both ending, not because modernity (culture driven by capital, economic forces, markets, and their colonization of every aspect of political and social life) had *failed*, but because it has *triumphed*. As an investigation of representation, modernism had had two wishes: to lead its viewers toward "the social reality of the sign" and to turn signs into their own "bedrock of World/Nature/Sensation/Subjectivity." To believe that representations might have force in the world, they had to have substance and authority as things, not illusions, and not even representations of other things. They had to be things whose function was embodied in their ability to work as structuring systems of signification. Modernism had to function critically in relation to representation in order to perform its critique of modernity.

To understand how the signifying activity of modernism functioned as a politics, Clark invokes the idea of "contingency" as the concept of social order without anchor or transcendent values. In such circumstances, socialism "was one of the forces, maybe *the* force, that made for the falsely polarized choice which modernism believed it had before it — between idealism and materialism, or *Ubermensch* and *lumpen*, or esoteric and popular." Without that organizing, oppositional structure, where are we? The strains of modernism that were allied with the socialist aspiration do not, of course, comprise the whole of modernism's aesthetic range, any more than aesthetic work defines the entirety of socialism's political activities. But belief in their powerful, mutually driven connection has been at the core of a particular tradition of art historical work. The "idea" to which Clark is bidding farewell is not socialism, but modernism, and the conviction that the choices it faced were framed as the opposition of esoteric to popular, negation to compromise. In that tradition, fine art's function was to oppose the culture industries, the totalitarian state, and the hegemony of modern capitalism through an avant-garde disruption of normative representation. In the face of historical realities, as Clark acknowledges, this has to be recognized as a false framing of the modernist project. So he offers a series of readings of paintings that show the ways representational strategies can be understood differently, as enacting the "disenchantment with the world" of modernity.

That disenchantment is certainly intensified in the current moment, and even if one reads the development and crux of modernism against the grain of both received traditions and Clark's reframing, those of us who ever imagined things might be other than they are derive little solace for the state in which we find ourselves now. The experiment of democracy hatched in the Enlightenment and the visions of socialism provoked in response to industrialization are in the throes — if not in the aftermath — of failure. Democracy is so broken that its parts no longer seem to fit together. The fundamental analysis on which socialism was conceived seems unfit for the challenges of contemporary life, too earnest and directed to address the systemic degradation of civil society, public good, or common sense (all notions that seem decorous and antiquated, a symptom of how much they are needed). The question is not how did we get here but what is the "here" at which we have arrived — so destructively far from rational thought or political-ecological realities that our very survival hangs in the balance. The fate of socialism seems a smaller matter compared to the grim future of a planetary ecology capable of sustaining human life, and yet, the two are interlinked. And thinking about the history of modernism as a tale of aspirations to set a path that could have been different, with a less dire outcome, is one we must engage with now and in the days to come. Looking at modernism as a history of how we got into this state might also be useful. The celebration of individualism and progress, complicity with commerce, cult of celebrity, creation of rarified commodities and consumable spectacles are all, also, inscribed across the corpus of modern painting. But first, back to *Farewell*.

Modernity is bereft, as Clark points out in his introduction, of the values that had driven religious art, courtly practice, monarchical or aristocratic patronage systems. Modern culture constructs a belief system from economics and the management of risk. The economic system of signs is a crucial piece of the theoretical armature, because money "is the root form of representation in bourgeois society." Modernity is driven by economic considerations, he says, and had no "compelling image or ritualization of purpose" outside of these conditions. This is not the same as describing a teleological fall from the grace of the sacred to the plane of the secular in cultural practices and institutions. Instead, it is a description of the removal of a frame of absolute beliefs and certainties that are replaced with contingencies. That term, and its multivalent possibilities, forms one of the key concepts of the book, and though autonomy, the usual term of modernism's self-definition as an aesthetic practice, gets less play, the two are entwined as myth and explanation of modernism's representation of itself to itself in works of art. Contingency describes the condition in which no givens, no *a priori* certainties or transcendent, absolute, value systems, can be depended upon as the ground of reception or production.

To get at this concept more concretely, Clark examines six "limit cases" in that history, through close studies of works by Jacques-Louis David, Lucien Pissarro, Paul Cézanne, Pablo Picasso, Kasimir

Malevich/Lazar "El" Lissitzky, and Jackson Pollock. He characterizes these as moments in which the "contingency" that characterizes modernism is exposed in representational activity. His six studies are different in length and kind, but they share certain methodological strengths. Each work is situated within arguments that muster evidence from carefully selected documents. The course of a day, the date of an exhibit, a moment of publication, a season of change, the particular temporalities, like the details of circumstance, are attended to with care. He reads these moments in the surfaces and structures of works of art, their particular demonstrations of ideas about what a painting might be — and in so being, expose some belief about the efficacy of works of art to perform ideas as instantiations. Or, to put it more simply, Clark shows how in their specific construction and production paintings perform ideas about what painting might be — and by extension, what representation shows us about the function of images as cultural objects embodying beliefs.

In standard critical studies of modern art, formal innovations and strategic disruptions are often characterized as "political" interventions into sign systems. These approaches are too literal for Clark, too close to the ideologies that produced them, to satisfy his inquiry. Thus he takes the common discussion of Cubism — as a way to represent a new way of seeing the world — and suggests that, at least in the period of 1912 on which he concentrates his study of Picasso's monochrome canvases, Cubism was not about representation. It was not about a painting in the service of visual epistemology, but instead, "a metaphorical admission of counterfeit." Cubism, Clark concludes, was not about an object world, but "a performance of contingencies at every point." The paintings fail to create a new language, and only pretend to do so. They are filled with "nothing but devices." Aesthetically beautiful, they are a demonstration, in Clark's reading, of the failure of painting to represent a way of seeing.

In Clark's account, modern painting is a play of procedures, not a language game or an activity of sign systems. He argues that modernism's philosophical moves question the way painting's means are used in their specificity. Pissarro's women standing out of the sun enact an anarchist worldview, or flirtation with it, through the painter's portrayal of labor and rest at the edge of a field. Picasso's layered (cubist) transparency obviates the referential world. Malevich's black square performs an act of negation that becomes the sign under which communism's non-objectivity will be made into a shared consciousness. And Pollock's paintings "about nothing" contest "bourgeois hegemony in the realm of consciousness." The construction of outsider-ness, the stance of the avant-garde, was frequently complicit, and Clark does not flinch from acknowledging Pollock's opportunism even as he holds onto the more potent weight of Malevich's negations. The conditions of War Communism are not those of postwar America, though the face of triumphalism is no prettier to look on than that of repression and horror. They are related in ways that are uncomfortable to admit.

Clark's technique relies on selectivity, exclusion, and oppositions. Critical attention to the "social reality of the sign," so marked in its import, depends upon picking some signs and not others. The "good" objects of his modernism are pitched against the "bad" or bad faith works — so David's portrait of Marat is posed against Joseph Roques's 1794 depiction of the same scene, Pissarro's *Two Young Peasant Women* (1892) against Jean-François Millet's *The Angelus* (1857), Picasso's *Woman with a Mandolin* (1910) against his own work in the previous years, Pollock's *Sea Change* against *Alchemy*, both painted in 1947. This was his approach in the magisterial *Painting of Modern Life*, where the selection of the "good" impressionist works were those critical of the deleterious effects of modern life in Paris and opposed to those whose depiction of idylls and entertainments is so characteristic of Impressionism writ large. Clark gives an account of the decisions that determined his studies in *Farewell*. Mapping his project across the six cases he chose for the book, Clark notes the long gap between the dates of the first and second study — David in 1793 and Pissarro in 1891. Gesturing to his other books and their contribution to that period, he acknowledges that his critics accuse him (somewhat justly, he admits) of not wanting to look at the long periods of "the true quiet — the true orderliness and confidence of bourgeois society in its heyday." His rejection of the "true quiet" hinges on a belief that all of modern painting — all that matters in modern painting, that is — is an outcry against the disastrous reality of modernity.

———

And here is where my description of Clark's project ends and questions about its premises arise. If we understand modernism only through those works that despised it, those artists whose output stood in a negative or negating relation to it, then do we provide ourselves with an adequate assessment of what occurred and what role fine art has played in its complicities? What alternative is there to the consensual narratives that propose that the function of aesthetic work is the power and legitimacy of critique? At stake is the question of how to formulate our understanding of the present, and future, of art as a category of cultural activity. To look again at modernism outside the (exclusionary) frames that allow it to be significant only when it stages a protest against modernity may be an unsavory process to those used to the version of that history that privileged the "esoteric" and oppositional. Much of modern art was conceived and practiced very differently, not as an opposition or negation, but instead, as an engagement with the institutions, drives, and forces of modernity. Think of Caspar David Friedrich's *Wanderer Above the Mists* (1817–'18), John Martin's crowd-pleasing spectacles of biblical scenes, Frederic Church's landscapes, George Bellows's boxing men, charged with the physicality and virility of an emerging nation, of Charles Sheeler's *River Rouge Plant*, Robert Delaunay's studies of the Eiffel Tower, or the portraits of Thomas Eakins, John Singer Sargent — the list could go on and on. These are celebratory paintings, not critical, and that needs to be addressed. To understand the political realities of signs, and roles of representations, we have to engage with their various complicities and compromises, alliances with ideologies, not only oppositions to them. Through their integration into modernity, they also provide useful material for reworking a specific idea of modernism. In the body of critical practices whose lineage tracks almost directly from early 20th-century debates about aesthetics and politics, too much was excluded from consideration. Like biologists whose attention was focused on a rarified species as if it were indicative, the art historians who subscribed to esoteric critique missed the complexities of the larger ecology. This is not a popular view in academic circles.

If we consider the broad spectrum of painting and image production in modernity, it might change the basic characterization of modernism, aesthetics, and arguments in and with representation. We see other ways images naturalize modes of representing — realism and naturalism, reportage and entertainment, celebritization and branding, commercialism and consumption, sentimentality and celebration — within the larger history of modernism. The potential of the sign to be a site of political struggle or of representation to be a thing in itself, an aspect of the material world, is only one part of its operation. Its capacities to produce a naturalized illusion, an absorbing experience among others, is another. Our current ecologies of knowledge require a suturing, however clumsy and inadequate, between the semiotics of representation and the material world at risk through its misrepresentation. But tasking fine art with the burden of fixing the broken world through a practice of esoteric critique may not be the way to preserve either aesthetics or humanity.

I am not posing these observations as a criticism of Clark or his work. I have no standing to do this. But the questions I am posing come from the fact that I never subscribed to the core belief that modernism was at its best (either aesthetically or morally) when it was focused on critique. Nor can I accept the unifying rhetoric of the term "modernism" as a rubric. The difficulty is that that version of modernism is what the art historians made of it (critical, oppositional), and that consensual narrative — however fine its arguments about representation and belief — is inadequate to the historical task of describing and explaining aesthetic activity, positing its function and identity. These other aspects of modernism, their bulk and volume, can't be shrugged off with an elite dismissal, as if they don't matter because they didn't do the "real" work, the sanctioned work, the true task of aesthetic ideology — which was somehow construed as performing critique. Much of modern art overtly reaffirmed commercialism, engaged popular and mass media cultures, became part of corporatization, and assisted in the global reach of colonizing systems of capital, of the info-entertainment industries that use the techniques of fashion, seduction, and consumption as their effective instruments. Modern art was a culture industry, not outside of or apart from the culture of modernity.

Modernism was not *an* idea, not a singular and well-formed position. The multiplicity and heterogeneity of its dimensions have to be addressed. Many of the robust aspects of modernism are ignored in the tradition of high academic art history: the traditions of reportage and journalistic modernism that arose in work of Americans, Winslow Homer, then the Ashcan School; the course of what might be termed "commercial" modernism, beginning with the scandal caused by John Everett Millais's contract with Pears' Soap for his *Bubbles* painting of 1886, but continuing into the partnerships forged between corporate culture and design — the transformation of the modern world into its very modernity. If Lissitzky's 1920 Propaganda board mounted in a street in Vitebsk is the voice of the state shouting through the revolution, as Clark so chillingly suggests, then what are we to make of the absorption of the lessons and forms of Lissitzky, by way of the Bauhaus, into the world of Paul Rand, IBM, and global systems of corporate capitalism? Do we dismiss these or look at them as formations of modernism and modernity? These are legitimate (and, for better or worse, legitimating) aspects of visual culture in the period of modernity in which industrialization, the rise of nation-states, systems of capital and labor, transformed Europe, Russia, and the United States so dramatically.

In the first decades of the 20th century, the affirmative tone of American modernism — with its celebration of construction sites, new bridges and train stations, love of steel construction, the subway, shop girls and immigrants — is a long way from critical attempts at disruption. John Sloan published his images in *The Masses*, and Ben Shahn depicted *Sacco and Vanzetti*, and efforts to support the organization of workers are everywhere evident in the early decades of 20th-century art, alongside the elevation of determined grit to the status of quintessential American spirit. Their direct and directed attempts to intervene in "the disenchantment of the world" and to alter the conditions that caused it are evident and embodied in their production, but the same can be said of Thomas Hart Benton's works, which have a radically different ideology.

A history of modernism based on only those works with an evident commitment to a project of social reform will always read as a failure. The goal "to imagine otherwise" that repeats as a leitmotif in Clark's works (not only this book) always assumes that the "otherwise" is a world remade with capital tamed, justice served, labor's interests addressed, and, perhaps, inequities of gender, class, education, and advantage redressed. These are all goals to which any sane person would subscribe. But it is not a description of modern art. Rather, it is a prescription for what modernism was supposed to do. Once feminism, queer activism, and civil rights add their own literal advocacy to the world of fine art, much of the allusive and performative activities of sign and surface, of feints of representation, and of strategies of epistemological reflection about the seen, unseen, and unseeable disappear in the banner and slogan protest art and iconographic struggles of identity politics. Didactic works do not lend themselves to the same kind of interpretative work; they direct our attention rather than calling us to engagement with their workings. The terms on which insight is produced experientially shift the bases of interpretation for many minimalist, conceptual, installation, and performance works. What might it mean to suggest an approach to works of art for their experiential rather than their critical activity?

How, for instance, do we discuss Anish Kapoor's *Cloud Gate*, a strikingly successful piece of public art mounted in Chicago's Millenium Park? A beautifully complex elliptoid of seamless steel plates with a mirrored surface, fondly referred to as a silver jelly bean, is a masterwork of technical craft and elegant form. Weighing more than a hundred tons and about three stories high, it creates intimacy rather than intimidation. All reflection, illusion, deception, all tricks of distortion and disoriented perception, it is a work that enchants, spellbinds. It has no outside, performs no exclusions. Its engagements are immediate, its defamiliarizations are without edge or threat. They perform an experiential opening into attention, to the activity of seeing and knowing, of belief and its grounds. How, it proposes, do we figure to ourselves within a landscape of sociality and public space? What locations are produced as assurance of our place in relation to others? How do we see ourselves — not what perception of a given self returns to us through vision, but how is the visual constructed to create a sense of self and of visuality as its means of construction? How do we know what we know and enter into the belief systems that either reinforce or reformulatethose beliefs? What ideas do we have now about art and its ability to perform some role in our lives?

Only a cynic would condemn the *Cloud Gate* on the basis of its universal appeal, characterize it as a sop to popular taste, a fun-house mirror meant to please the uncritical appetites of the bourgeoisie and their petted offspring. If the *Cloud Gate* functions — as it does — through direct engagement, appeal, immediacy, without the distance of criticality, and yet, performs its aesthetic operations in that generative place between formal qualities and sustained engagement, in the never-ending irresolution of the relation between what it is and what it does, its identity and its activity — then what aesthetic principles can be generated from it as a work of art? How are the belief systems that formed premises for understanding the past history of modernism rethought if *Cloud Gate* belongs, as it irrefutably does, in that lineage. Behind *Cloud Gate*, in simple formal terms, are Arp and Brancusi, the mirrored halls of palaces, the public fountains of Rome and Paris, the monumental scale of Gehry's polished surfaces, the threat and phenomenological complexity of Richard Serra's forms, and so on — as well as the entertainment spaces of amusement parks and boardwalk sideshows. The modernism of engagements, an aesthetic of experience, of attention called rather than directed, has many dimensions to it long left out of the canon created by those guided by a principle of "critique" and negation, a stance of moral superiority and outsider positions, or exclusionary selectivity that ignored the larger fuller field of art production at its peril. That peril is ours, in a perilous world whose fate hangs upon a different kind of intellectual engagement with the production of illusion and belief.

The assumption that at its core modernism was committed to redressing the horrors wrought by modernity is a belief we cannot afford — it neither explains the extent to which other forces of representation were at work, in some cases all too successfully, nor provides an alternative. This attitude condemns us to the failure of art as directed energy, as the moral conscience of the culture, the site for and instrument of a realization that the world is broken and we must fix it. That last statement is all too true. But the belief that aesthetic activity is circumscribed by that task is neither accurate nor useful. Directed energy will never call us to attention. Prescriptive approaches limit the imaginative possibilities of works of art. Oppositional tactics are always reactive. We have to realize that negative notions, like the bankrupt ideas of critique, don't offer a way forward. They keep us at a superior distance from reality. We need to formulate a modernism of engagement founded in a recognition of complicity — ours and its — with the machinations and values according to which we live. ⁄

Second Nature

ANDREW NANCE

With so much to say on
nothing, and nothing to say
on plenty, I struck forth
with some errancy about my limbs —
"some spirit" in its window.
All hands to deck drifting
in half-subsumed arrogance
(wherein necks rock empty —
a pin on leaf pointing north)
and I, paraphrasing comfort, drew
up my mouth by drawstring
and left the porch. There was,
all about me, a sentinel of means
looking back at its own
signal — that mouthwash taste
of distilled outcome
residing in an investment
solidly perched on its negation —
I felt I was looking through it.

As "modern positivism
consigns it to poetry," so an "it"
remains the "anything" of no
thing that cannot remain
and I sensed, as lunches were
taken on the balcony with
regularity, that my task was
to speak to some residue
not of nature but of the absent
mythology of effort
through which taste, like rain,
is the sudden regression

of interpolation into dexterous
art. If little counterfeit
howls claim their ready-made
miscarriages — as in a *Très Riches
Heures*' "metaphysics of beauty
(in Plotinus, for instance)" —
then the end implicit in beauty
is the absolute currency
we hold time to (like waiting on
the train or waking just before
the alarm calls out).

Theophilus' regency calls it
a kind of present-perfect
as in a perpetual past, and though
some are gearing up for
change in weather unlike
weather, they know neither their
own half-life nor their
pocket's lasting virtue —
rain always rotating through
the day on a periodic
spectrum we were convinced of
by St. Paul's accent. Late
strolls through present
Greece make us weep
into our jacket's Water-Wicking
sleeve — tired of life
proceeding without stops
for art's less-than-natural
neutrality — I felt, stepping
from my door to drive,
that a cool debt was moving
through me as sun
warmed my soft-shelled
skull and left itself under late-
trimmed fingernails.

Then cries I always mistake
for owls occurred in a
kind of backwards time
like tomorrow's Sunday –
just as leaving a porch
in the morning makes
it mine because all retreats
into labor own their
interrogative artifice –
rain continually retreating
out of itself, or how in
packing my lunch I planned
not for a meal but for
a moment's reprieve inside
the day's terminal sun-
spotted center chamber.
Of course I tired preemptively
of noon's elongated jounce
as I was already fixated
on the day's derivative:
"This is one way to say
that affection hinges on displacement" or "There's
no warning sign that isn't
already cornering itself
through preservation" –
one way's elongation set
at right angle to another's
paucity makes it political
insofar as it sutures
change to apocalypse.

In polls, in perfunctory
insights about change's aid
to "life in the future," we
dare it to arrive from out
of the past and try, we taunt,

to take us back to gathering
what we live on on our own
time — as to divide one's
time is to incite a calumny
wherein fact becomes
an integer's plainspoken
positive misprision: mis-
matched socks on the opposite
feet, or feet we nailed to one
another mistaking our own
magistrature for a cross.

While I would not for some
comfort come clean — smoke
parsing wind as the wind
navigates mostly its own
parallel termini — but rather
look preoccupied for moment's
sake — so in moments'
exhalations, I would keep
reaching out for a foretelling,
some out-of-the-way truth
that neither smears
my window with light nor
washes itself of pollen it lives
through. "I know now"
forestalls iterations of some
disquiet while others move
like boots through a morning's
planetary luster: not knowing
and yet hoping, not knowing
and yet desiring some
willing martyr out of nature
for nature — a glass eye gazing
at everything at once, and
the orbit around
the center I left behind
on the porch's wetted pallet. ⁄⁄

IT'S A MISTAKE TO MISTAKE CONTENT FOR CONTENT

KENNETH GOLDSMITH

RECENTLY I WAS in the mood to listen to the music of the American mid-century composer Morton Feldman. I dug into my MP3 drive, found my Feldman folder, and opened it up. Amongst the various folders in the directory was one labeled "The Complete Works of Morton Feldman." I was surprised to see it there; I didn't remember downloading it. Curious, I looked at its date — 2009 — and realized that I must've grabbed it during the heyday of MP3 sharity blogs. I opened it to find 79 albums as *zipped* files. I unzipped three of them, listened to part of one, and closed the folder. I haven't opened it since.

My experience with Feldman indicates how, in a time when cultural artifacts are abundantly available, our primary focus has migrated from use to acquisition; I have more MP3s than I'll ever be able to listen to in the next 10 lifetimes, yet I compulsively keep downloading more. In this way our role as librarians and archivists has outpaced our role as cultural consumers. Engaging with media in a traditional sense is often the last thing we do, that is (like my Feldman experience), if we ever get to it at all. In the digital ecosystem, the apparatuses surrounding the artifact are more engaging than the artifact itself. Management (acquisition, distribution, archiving, filing, redundancy) is the cultural artifact's new content. *Context* is the new content. In an unanticipated twist to John Perry Barlow's 1994 prediction that in the digital age we'd be able to enjoy wine without the bottles, we've now come to prefer the bottles to the wine.

Back in 1983, the media critic and philosopher Vilém Flusser (1920–1991) described this exact phenomenon in a little book called *Towards a Philosophy of Photography*. Flusser claimed that the content of any given photograph is actually the camera that produced it. He continued with a series of nested apparatuses: the content of the camera is the programming that makes it function; the content of the programming is the photographic industry that produces it; and the content of the photographic industry is the military-industrial complex in which it is situated, and so forth. He viewed photography from a completely technical standpoint. In Flusser's view, the traditional content of the cultural artifact is completely subsumed by the apparatuses — technical, political, social, and industrial — surrounding, and thereby defining, it.

Although he was writing about analog, print-based photography, Flusser's ideas go a long way to explain our changing relationship to the cultural artifact in the digital age, reminding us of Moholy-Nagy's prediction that "those who are ignorant in matters of photography will be the illiterates of tomorrow."

The mistake most make in reading Flusser is to assume that he's talking about photography. Yes, he is, but that's the least relevant part. Imagine, instead, that everything he's saying about photography he's saying about the digital. This requires an act of imaginative translation on our part, but once you make that leap, you realize that this 1983 text astonishingly directly addresses our situation some three decades later. For instance, Flusser claimed that the camera was the ancestor of apparatuses, which are in the process of "robotizing all aspects of our lives, from one's most public acts to one's innermost thoughts, feelings, and desires." And when we look at social media — from blogs, to Twitter, to Facebook, and to Instagram — we can see he was correct. The Twitter game is like Wittgenstein's language games; we must learn the rules in order to play. Obeying such rules — going with the apparatus instead of against it — results in victories, substantiated by gains in followers and retweets. Failure to follow the rules (there are no official rules, actually, only a set of community-based standards that most players unquestioningly follow) results in isolation: loss of followers and tweets that go unretweeted. When we tweet, the 140-character constraint determines the form of our content, forcing us to tailor/robotize our production in order to comply with the Twitter apparatus.

Like the camera, the Twitter apparatus coerces/seduces us to tweet, and we dutifully obey. Once we're hooked into the game, we become compulsive: the more we tweet, the more we enrich the program, thereby increasing its standing within the larger social media apparatus and, ultimately, boosting Twitter's share price. In Flusserian terms, it doesn't really matter what we tweet (content); it just matters that we keep tweeting (apparatus). In his thinking, Flusser was obviously influenced by McLuhan's medium as message, but we can read this through the digital: when McLuhan claims that the "content of any medium is always another medium," Flusser might reframe this as "the content of any medium is always the series of apparatuses that produced it."

In fact, content plays no role whatsoever in Flusser's writing. A photograph is not a carrier of memories — your baby pictures are interchangeable with a million other baby pictures — but a predetermined artifact spit out by the camera apparatus. The camera is a voracious, greedy device, programmed to stalk images the way an animal stalks prey: the camera smells blood and (literally) snaps. Like Twitter, the more you shoot, the more you become addicted to the photographic apparatus, which Flusser likens to opium addiction or being on a "photograph-trip." In the end, you end up working for the camera and the industry that produced it. The more people who use an apparatus, the more feedback the company receives about its camera, the smarter it becomes, drawing more users to its base, thereby increasing the manufacturer's bottom line. For this reason, Instagram keeps adding new filter sets and features in order to retain and broaden its user base. To Instagram, the content of the photos people are taking is beside the point; the real point is that they keep taking them in order to fortify the apparatus.

Photography is easy. Anyone can push a button and produce a photograph without having a clue as to the inner workings of a camera. A lens on a camera will inevitably take telescopic photos. The program of the camera overrides the artifact that it produces. The programmers of cameras strive to keep their interfaces as simple as possible, to discourage experimentation outside of its parameters. The simple interface keeps the photographer pushing the button so they can produce, in Flusser's words, "more and more redundant images." The free cost of digital photography keeps the photographer playing the photographic game. (How many people snapping photos with a smartphone only take one shot of any given scene?) Those photos are uploaded to the cloud, where ever-more-redundant photos are stored. Your photo of the

Flatiron Building on Flickr is identically redundant to the millions already stored on Flickr, yet you keep on snapping them (just as I keep downloading MP3s).

The camera doesn't work for us. We work for the camera. Our compulsive behavior leaves no scene undocumented. I shoot therefore I am. Or as The Kinks put it, "People take pictures of each other / Just to prove that they really existed." When we take a holiday to a foreign country, the photos don't show the sights we saw, they show us the places where the camera has been and what it's done there. We think we're documenting our own memories, but what we're actually producing is memories for the apparatus. The digital photograph's metadata — geotagging, likes, shares, user connectivity, and so on — proves much more valuable to Instagram than any subject matter it captures. The image is irrelevant in comparison to the apparatuses surrounding it.

Once we buy into a specific apparatus, it's awfully hard to leave it. Your cultural artifact is locked within that system, constrained by its programming. Notice how another user's Instagram photo can't be resized, emailed, or downloaded to your hard drive. It can't exist within any other ecosystem than Instagram's.[1] Notice how easily Instagram can be integrated into the interface of its parent company, Facebook, but how difficult it is to share on Twitter, a competitor's platform. While we play the Instagram game by liking and reposting photos, the apparatus knows otherwise: a "like" is a way for the shareholder to verify that there are consumers populating the program; the greater and more verifiable the user base, the more valuable the apparatus.[2]

The physical value even of a printed photograph is negligible: it's just a piece of paper with information on it — cheap, ubiquitous, unstable, and infinitely reproducible. As opposed to a painting, where the value of the object resides in its singularity, the value of a photograph lies in the information on its surface. Its surface is ephemeral and, in the digital age, rewritable. The photograph is a pivotal artifact, bridging the industrial and postindustrial, embodying the transition from the physical to the purely informational. How that information is distributed determines much of its meaning.

In a paper-bound economy, its ubiquity in physical space was its distributive metric. But even then, the content in a poster or handbill was somewhere other than its image. Flusser writes, "The poster is without value; nobody owns it, it flaps torn in the wind yet the power of the advertising agency remains undiminished […]." Depending upon context and distribution, the paper-bound image could take on different meanings. Unlike, say, an image of a rocket ship glued to a television screen, a photograph of a rocket ship published in a newspaper could be clipped, stuffed into an envelope, and sent to a friend. Available to be passed hand-to-hand, the movable photographic artifact anticipated our vast image-sharing networks.[3]

The camera resembles a game of chess. It contains what appears to be an infinite number of possibilities, but in the end, those possibilities are prescribed by its programming. Just as every possible move and permutation of a chess game has long been exhausted, so too has every program of the camera. In the case of Instagram, with a user base of over 400 million, the programs are instantly exhausted, resulting in updates to the program that include new features in order to retain users. Although finite, the apparatus must always give the illusion of infinity in order to make each user feel that they can never exhaust the program. Or as Flussser says, "Photographs permanently displacing one another according to a program are redundant precisely because they are always 'new' […]." Your cell phone still makes calls, but you'd be foolish to think that it is about being a telephone in the same way that you'd be foolish to think that Instagram is about expressive photography.

BILL JACOBSON
INTERIM PORTRAIT #104, 1992
CHROMOGENIC PRINT
COURTESY OF THE ARTIST AND JULIE SAUL GALLERY, NEW YORK

After Flusser, the photo criticism of Sontag or Barthes, each of whom mostly ignores the apparatus in favor of the artifact, appears to miss the point entirely. Their achingly beautiful literary readings of the photograph as *memento mori* or studies in *studium* and *punctum* have no place in the Flusserian universe. While Sontag makes pronouncements like, "Photography is an elegiac art, a twilight art. Most subjects photographed are, just by virtue of being photographed, touched with pathos," Flusser counters that readings like Sontag's are simply more fodder for the apparatus:

> A number of human beings are struggling against this automatic programming [...] attempting to create a space for human intention in a world dominated by apparatuses. However, the apparatuses themselves automatically assimilate these attempts at liberation and enrich their programs with them.

The only hope? Those who attempt to break the system by doing something with the camera that was never intended by industry: Thomas Ruff, who took intentionally boring portraits or enlarged JPEGs to monumental scale, thereby exploiting their crappy resolution; or the blurred portraits of Bill Jacobson, so intentionally out of focus that the head of the subject resembles little more than a blot. Twitter is trickier to break. Attempts at self-reflexive critique within the Twitter apparatus such as @Horse_ebooks are instantly absorbed by the apparatus and celebrated by the corporation to highlight the diversity and playfulness of its expanded user base (once again making the company a more valuable entity). Again, the Twitter apparatus "automatically assimilates these attempts at liberation and enriches their programs with them."

I recall a few years ago, a prominent art historian asked me to join a reading group focused on media and communications studies. She was sensing that in order to be able to understand art being made in a post-digital time, literary-based models of art criticism (Krauss, Buchloh, *October*, etc.) would only get us so far. In order to understand contemporary culture, we needed to move from the artifact to the apparatus. So she proposed getting together and reading people like Flusser, Kittler, Groys, Manovich, Galloway, Sterne, Dean, Gitelman, and Parikka. The effect was profound and immediate. Suddenly, much of the new art and literature found a receptive framework and history that could speak to the networked conditions of the digital age.

In Flusser, we've found our Wittgenstein. By that I mean, in the ways that 1960s conceptual artists found his *Philosophical Investigations* as granting them the necessary permission to see the world around them with fresh eyes, Flusser's forays into media have framed, theorized, and unpacked the new complexities of our digital world. By empirically questioning received knowledge and recasting it within crisp lines of history and logic, he's made the digital legible in a time when its theorization is occluded and murky to say the least. Like de Kooning's famous statement: "History does not influence me. I influence it," it's taken Flusser's analog-based investigations in the 20th century to show us how to be in the digitally soaked 21st. ⁄⁄

ENDNOTES

1. Of course one could screen cap every Instagram on one's feed and save it to disc, but doing so would be to orphan that artifact; stripped of its apparatus, the image would lose much of its meaning.

2. One only need remember Ello, the social network that grew as quickly as it could, populating its shell with as many users as it could garner, only to be flipped as soon as possible. It was selling its enormous user base, not its "content."

3. We could also say that file-sharing networks later permitted the sharing of that television show, but in its entirety, not a single image. In order to extract a single image from TV, you had to invoke the photographic model and shoot it off the TV screen, thereby turning it into a photograph.

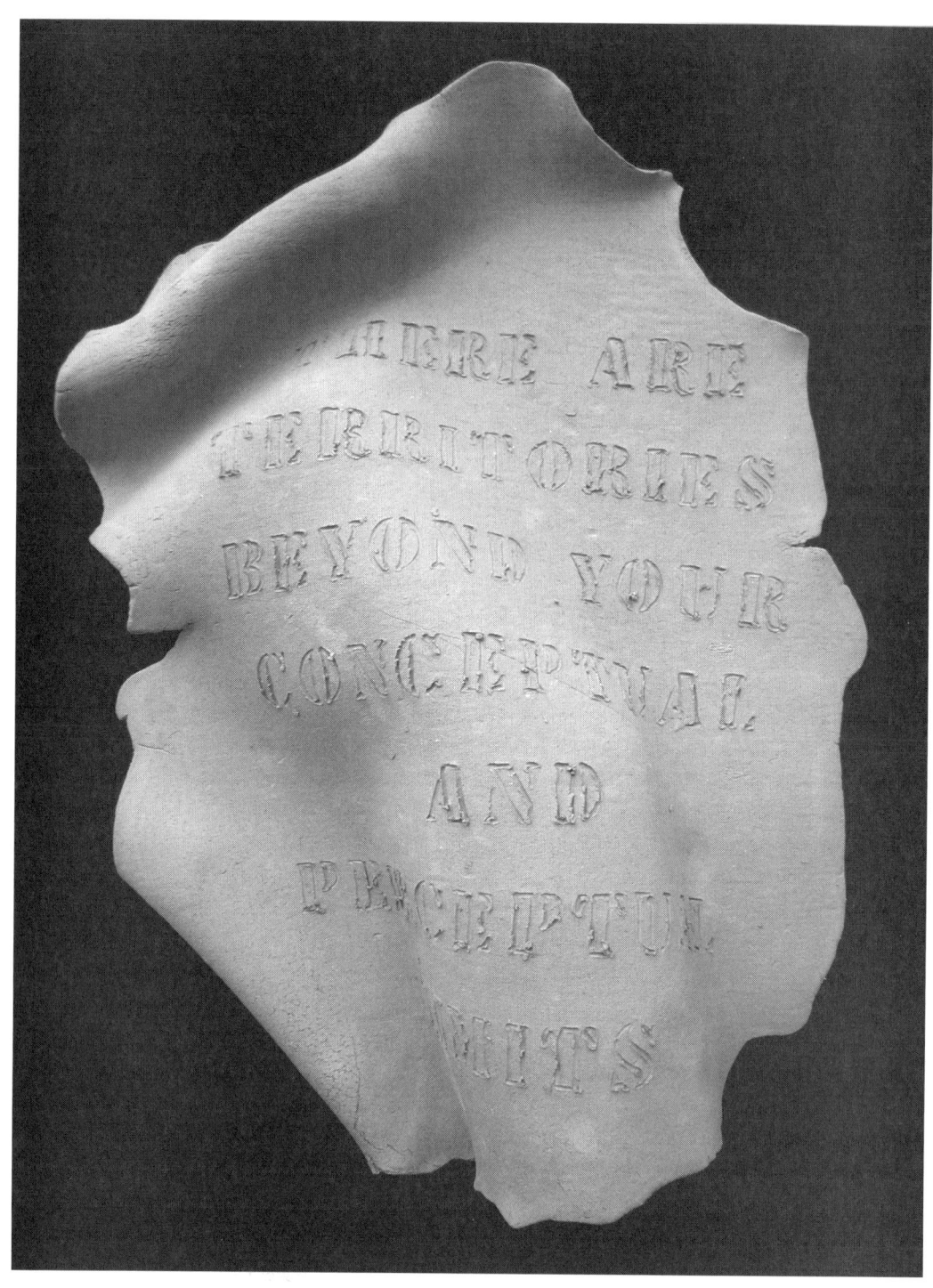

ANNA MAYER
THERE ARE TERRITORIES BEYOND YOUR CONCEPTUAL AND PERCEPTUAL LIMITS (TROPICAL TERRACE),
FROM THE FIREFUL OF FEAR PROJECT, 2008–ONGOING
WILDFIRE-FIRED CERAMIC (FORTHCOMING), 19 3/4 x 15 1/2 x 3"
COURTESY OF THE ARTIST

THE PEOPLE DOWNSTAIRS

DIANA FUSS

THE "NO CRISIS" SERIES asks us to think about the interpretative work of the humanities. Doing so has made me think about a broader topic: the interpretive work of being human.

It was a late summer night when my elderly mother called the police to report a man in her basement. They responded in force but found no evidence of an intruder lurking behind the furnace. That night might have offered up just another zany Mom story (the latest in a long and entertaining history) had my mother not asked the officers on their way out: "The man — don't you see him? He's standing right next to you." It was off to the emergency room for her, where she was eventually diagnosed with chronic dehydration and UTI, a urinary tract infection common in elderly women and known to make one more than a little loopy. A one-two punch of antibiotics and rehab will bring her back to baseline and back to her old self, the doctor assured us. Unless, he added casually, her baseline was actually dementia and the infection simply made the neurocognitive disorder worse — only time will tell. *Say what?*

One year, two hospitalizations, and months of in-home elder care later, my mother's "baseline" has become more obvious and her basement a whole lot more crowded. As the weather turned cold her imaginary subterranean dweller brought his whole family to gather around the warmth of her furnace. Lately he has ventured upstairs late at night to sit on my mother's recliner, keeping watchful company as she sleeps. In return, she leaves blankets and food for "the people downstairs," helping them survive in greater comfort. It's a Dickensian tale writ small, playing out in the mind of a kind, befuddled woman no longer able to remember her children's names but determined to help a hungry and homeless family.

My mother's dementia did not appear overnight. The signs had been there, but neither myself nor my siblings — despite our combined learning, despite my own training in interpretation — knew quite how to read them: some rotting food in the refrigerator, occasional dirty clothes on the floor, and (we eventually discovered) months of unpaid bills, undeposited checks, and an expired credit card. She had lost some weight, but that appeared to be a good thing. She wasn't telephoning her children anymore, but when we asked why she explained she was quite busy. When her speech problems emerged, along with an inability to remember names, we wondered if that mysterious fall last year was actually a small stroke. We had a dozen reasonable explanations for her changes in personality and odd behavior. Dementia had never crossed our minds.

So it came as a shock when her general care practitioner informed us that indeed my mother had dementia and she needed immediate round-the-clock supervision. She should not be allowed to walk unaccompanied (what if she fell?), nor should she be alone at night (again, what if she fell?). Had we considered assisted living or a nursing home? The message was delivered with all the subtlety of a judge's gavel: "the name of the game is safety," and it was time for we children to wake up, take control, and decide our mother's future. A crisis was at hand.

How did Mom feel about all this? She certainly didn't feel she was "in crisis." Nor did she feel or behave like an invalid. Overall, her lifestyle was, and still is, a happy and healthy one. She spends her mornings eating nutritious brunches and perusing the newspaper, her afternoons reading magazines or napping, and her evenings enjoying all things HGTV. The center of her day, and reason for getting up in the morning, is her beloved dog Daisy, whose companionship gives her unending joy. Aside from some benign hallucinations and not so benign anxiety late in the day (known as "sundowning"), she likes her life and cherishes her independence. At this point she welcomes help with bills and food shopping, generally manages her day with no trouble, and hates being patronized. *Hello, hello* she chastises every time a doctor presumes to talk over her head to address us instead. *I'm right here.*

My mother is not unaware of what is happening to her — her loss of memory, difficulty with names, confusion with numbers, bouts of agitation. Sometimes even she wonders if those people taking up residence in the basement might be delusions. Most heartbreaking to me are her moments of absolute clarity: "I'm me but I'm not me." Yet, while her "not me" moments have sometimes made her more anxious, they have not made her suddenly helpless. So who are we to take her independence away from her? Is either assisted living (which she can't afford) or nursing home living (which she can't imagine) really the best or only option? Why should safety be prioritized over everything else, including happiness? Is an institutional life of restricted physical mobility, reduced personal liberties, and rigid daily schedules — in other words, a world stripped of all life's homier pleasures — really worth living?

In the midst of our fretful family conversations, Atul Gawande's *Being Mortal: Medicine and What Matters in the End* arrived like a gift from the elder care gods. If such a class of divinities existed, Gawande, a Boston cancer surgeon and staff writer for *The New Yorker*, would be a modern Apollo, Greek god of both healing and poetry and an oracle deserving of the name. Winner of a MacArthur "genius" fellowship, Gawande plays for high stakes. All four of his published books address ambiguous medical situations and what to do about them, whether it's how to deal with surgical surprises (*Complications*), how to make sound life and death decisions (*Better*), or how to use simple checklists to avoid harming others or ourselves (*The Checklist Manifesto*). *Being Mortal*, which brings a bracing levelheadedness to complicated end-of-life questions, is his latest and most successful attempt to show doctors how to stop making preventable mistakes, and patients how to start making informed decisions. It's a winning combo.

Gawande is a terrific writer with a rare gift: communicating hard truths in a way people can actually hear. This talent is on full display in *Being Mortal*, a beautifully conceived, remarkably helpful, and unexpectedly delightful book on the realities of infirmity and old age. Gawande has a powerful message for doctors and patients alike: even the frailest among us have the right to live a fulfilling, satisfying life right up to our last dying breath. And for the families of those too weak and infirm to continue as they have, his message is even more pointed: our role is not to take away our loved one's options but to determine how he or she wants to live given their limitations. The choice must be theirs; our job is to do what we can, within our own limitations, to make that wish a reality.

Such advice may sound commonsensical, even obvious, but it is rarely heeded. People have always hoped to die where they live, but, as Gawande notes, by the 1980s only 17 percent of deaths occurred in the home. In the past half-century the majority of Americans died in nursing homes or hospitals, largely because advances in science have led us all to believe that mortality is fundamentally no longer a human experience but a medical one. Even now, despite the rise of hospice facilities, in-home care, and other attempts to make humane improvements to end-of-life treatment, we are far more likely to die amongst medical professionals than our own family. Gawande acknowledges that historically there is no better time than the present to be old. But it is not at all clear that there is no better time to die. Dying away from home and surrounded by strangers is hardly anyone's definition of a good death.

Some readers may be surprised to learn that dying of old age is actually a relatively new historical experience. Gawande explains that as recently as 200 years ago death rarely waited for the natural wearing down of the body and its attendant loss of muscle mass, lung capacity, and motor neurons. You were lucky to make it to age 30 at a time when dying of old age was an uncommon event, and the elderly, as a result, were deeply revered. Now, as the average life span in America zooms past 80, we have in effect lived well beyond our expiration dates, and the end is not yet in sight. According to the government's 2010 census, the elderly population will double in the next 35 years.

Are we prepared to care for so many aging citizens? Not even close. The most startling fact reported in *Being Mortal*, a book that responsibly takes pains to marshal its evidence, is that while the number of seniors in this country has grown exponentially, the number of geriatricians has actually fallen (more than 25 percent in the past couple of decades). To his great credit, Gawande, who also teaches at Harvard Medical School, gives a completely candid diagnosis of how and why medical schools are failing the elderly: geriatrician incomes are amongst the lowest in medicine; doctors tend not to appreciate patients who compromise their reputations as skilled healers by routinely dying on them; old people, who may be deaf, blind, forgetful, or just plain ornery, can be tough to work with and take up considerable office time; and end-of-life care is not exactly the sexiest field in modern medicine, lacking the star power of specialties like cardiology or plastic surgery. Perhaps the greatest culprit is that in a culture that worships youth, nobody, not even a doctor, enjoys constant reminders of the stark reality of aging and the inevitability of mortality. Ninety-seven percent of medical school graduates have not taken even a single course in geriatrics, which is why it's already too late to produce a new generation of geriatricians to handle the tsunami of elder care coming our way. Thankfully though, Gawande does have an elegant solution: send some of our current specialists in geriatrics into every medical school, nursing school, and school of social work to train a whole range of medical professionals to begin working together to provide quality healthcare for one of our most vulnerable population groups.

The average American spends a year or more of their so-called golden years in a nursing home — the very name enough to inflict terror in people of any age. To this day my image of a nursing home is colored by May Sarton's deeply affecting 1973 novel *As We Are Now*, an unforgettable and chilling portrait of the sad indignities of living and dying in a home for the aged. Spurred on by the birth of Medicare and Medicaid in 1965, the nursing home was America's answer to the horrors of the almshouse, charitable dumping grounds for the poor and the elderly. But Sarton viewed the soon-infamous "Park and Die" facilities as no different than other failed institutions: they are jails only worse since there is no hope for release; they are orphanages where accidental falls are treated as misdemeanors and punishment comes in repeated acts of infantilization; and they are asylums where everyday emotions like anger or irritation are immediately read as symptoms of senility. In Sarton's self-proclaimed *J'accuse*, the nursing home is our national shame: "a concentration camp for the old."

Sarton melodramatically ends her novel with the elderly protagonist deliberately blowing up her nursing home, with herself and everyone else in it. Surely there are better ways to make a dreary and dismal institution disappear. Gawande is somewhat reassuring on today's nursing homes, which he believes are not the Dickensian places they used to be. Even the poor, he writes, can expect from a nursing home regular meals, doctor visits, and physical therapy. But are such anemic environments really adequate? Do they feed the soul or stimulate the imagination? What could be worse at the end of a full life than losing all privacy, not to mention control over things we have always taken for granted, like when to wake in the morning, take a shower, go for a walk, or retire to bed? Institutions are institutions. They run according to the convenience and schedules of the professionals who work there, not the people they serve.

And here is where Gawande's brave and lucid book shines most. Despite the best of intentions and a wealth of dedicated and compassionate medical caregivers, we have somehow produced homes for the aged that bear no resemblance at all to what we normally call living. Sure, physical safety is important, but the medical mania for keeping the elderly from ambulating and possibly breaking a hip can actually restrict and impoverish a life rather than bolster or extend it. It's not the mere fact of existence that brings true purpose to our lives but rather our lifelong loves and interests, our hobbies and habits, our pets and our family. Why do we assume, Gawande reasonably asks, that the only question that matters in elder care is how to keep the aged safe rather than the more meaningful question of how to make their lives worth living? Forced participation in sing-alongs or crafts, be they in nursing homes or the unfortunately named Adult Day Care Centers, may well have a number of cognitive or psychological benefits for those who enjoy them, but it isn't how I would like to spend my final years. Like my mother, I hope to keep reading or listening to audio books, enjoy slow meals, care for my pets, write if I can, and spend as much time with family and close friends as possible. If Gawande's sane and sensible book translates into actual policy, we might all someday be able to control our own thermostats or get up and go to bed exactly when we want. Why should any of us have to give up being a real person, no matter how brittle our bones may be? Gawande's philosophy is simple: "Let frail elderly people maintain as much control over their care as possible, instead of having to let their care control them."

Make no mistake about it, in its own quiet and generous way Gawande's latest book is no less a call to arms than his previous *The Checklist Manifesto*. The right to retain one's personhood should never stop at the nursing home door. It's not in fact too late to establish more affordable in-home care for seniors who need it, or to transform even the most sterile nursing homes into places that are more than mere shelters or way stations to the beyond. In *Being Mortal*'s most inspiring chapter, Gawande tells the story of an upstate New York nursing home director who suddenly realizes that the missing ingredient in nursing home life is life itself. To give his residents something to live for he offers them something to care for: rabbits and hens outside the home, two dogs and four cats inside the home, and a parakeet in every room. He plants vegetable and flower gardens on the lawn to bring in the seasons. And he establishes on-site playgrounds, childcare, and after-school programs to bring family life into the facility. This one visionary doctor had the brilliant idea to put the "home" back into "nursing home." The results of his revolution were dramatic: mortality rates fell 15 percent annually and drug expenses fell to a mere 38 percent of comparable costs at peer institutions (thanks in particular to the reduced use of antipsychotic drugs like Haldol to treat anxiety and agitation). It is perhaps unsurprising to be given notice that the elderly and infirm, needing more than a roof over their heads and food on the table, crave normal lives and a reason to live. What is truly remarkable is that it has taken the rest of us so long to finally read the memo.

Exactly how has a surgeon's book on the bleak subject of end-of-life care (a book still on *The New York Times* hardcover bestseller list after more than a year) managed to bring both sound medical science and humane practical solutions to one of the most painful and delicate conversations any family is likely to face? Gawande has succeeded in large part by bringing a humanist perspective to a problem assumed to be simply medical or technological. While some scientists have dismissed the humanities for the apparent sins of subjective thinking and uncertain grounds, Gawande intuits exactly how much medical research needs humanistic inquiry if we are truly to understand what living a life, even in extremis, actually means. *Being Mortal*, a book chock-full of important scientific information, also reads like an absorbing short story collection, with interlinked dramas taking up the great themes of modern literature (life, death, love, family). Historical knowledge, cultural awareness, personal empathy, and ethical action inform every chapter, as Gawande gently persuades us that our personal journeys into that good night will never simply be a matter of what medications to take or institutions to live in.

Reading this profoundly humanistic science book on aging makes me wonder if the intellectual work of the humanities, the study of what makes us human, has always been a bit like old age. Close reading, careful listening, and patient thinking (often about complex subjects that indeed rarely have clear answers) are deeply reflective practices that slow us down and educate not just our minds but also our emotions. In *Being Mortal*, Gawande engages in all three critical practices, returning to the core Aristotelian question that founded the humanities: what is a good life? It is the humanist in the scientist who recognizes that "living is a kind of skill." At the same time, it is the scientist in the humanist who reminds us "old age is not a diagnosis." In this book, the sciences and the humanities are neither at war nor in crisis. They are in intimate and productive collaboration.

Being Mortal draws on the strengths of both the humanities and the sciences to demonstrate one of life's harder lessons: how to really listen to someone and how to ask the right questions in the first place. Now, as my mother's dementia progresses, we are becoming appreciative close readers of the stories she shares. Every tall tale, every fictitious memory, every hallucination tells us something important about what makes her uneasy and what makes her happy. The strange man in the basement who increasingly keeps her company while she sleeps tells us that she is afraid to be alone at night. But from her description of this man we can also see that she takes enormous solace in the company of a ghost bearing a distinct resemblance to the father who once doted on his only child and made her feel safe. My mother is a storyteller — that is her truth. As her life narrows she invents stories that help her to not only hold on to the values and activities she finds deeply meaningful but also restore to her world the people and things she has lost. We should all have such a gift.

In the end my siblings and I followed Gawande's sage advice and asked my mother what she wants to do now that she needs more help. Six years ago my mother moved into my New Jersey home and stayed several years as she recovered from hip and knee surgery. Regaining her health and wanting her independence back, she returned to Cape Cod, where my nearby brother and his family took a turn helping her manage the demands of living alone. Now that her infirmities have become more debilitating, my sister has stepped up and answered the call, buying a new home with her own retirement in mind and creating an attached in-law space. My mother is thrilled to soon be moving to Down East Maine and spending more time with her eldest daughter and family. Such a choice may not be for everyone; Gawande's research reveals that most elderly parents do not wish to live with their children, and they can still feel lonely or anxious when they do. But while my mother may have dementia, she has been utterly clear about her priorities: she doesn't wish to be by herself anymore, but nor does she want institutional living (bingo and socials, she says, are not for her). She wants to decide for herself how to spend her time, organize her meals, and walk her dog, and she's willing to risk accidental falls to do it. Her deepest wish at the end of her life is simply to be, and preferably in the company of family close by. Turns out that the one thing that makes her life most worth living is us. ◢

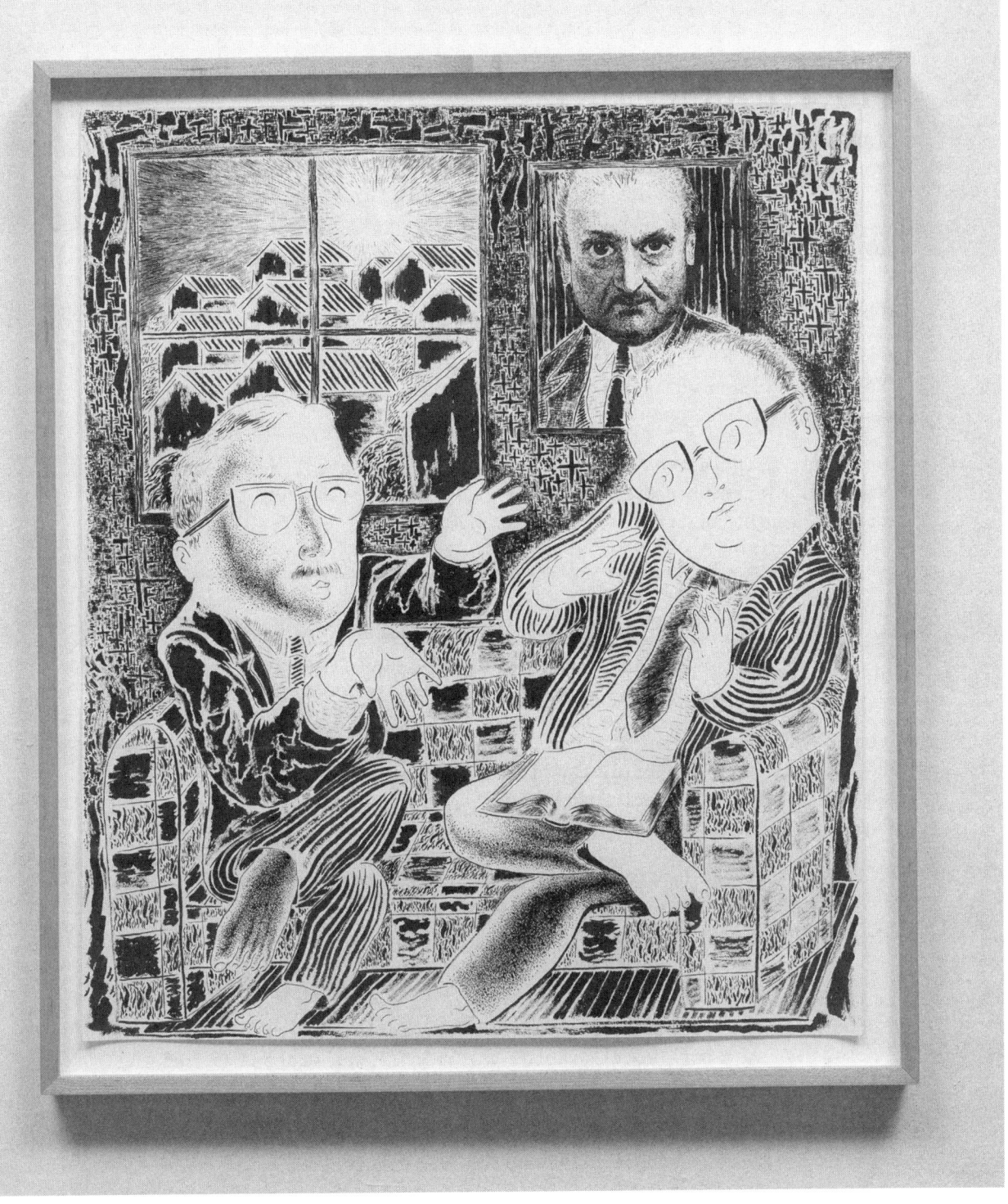

JOSH MANNIS
HUBERT DREYFUS AND BRYAN MAGEE DISCUSS HEIDEGGER, 2015
INK ON PAPER, 25 1/2 X 22"
COURTESY OF THE ARTIST

For Hunger

MARGARET RONDA

Yesterday was nothing, empty-handed. Today was a dream, she appeared at the door with a bag of fruit she could not eat. Yesterday I was at ocean's edge and her hand ebbed from mine. To gag, to heave, to swallow deep.

A nothing full of planes and cars. One parked in the patch of roses and insisted. I measured speech in streams of escalating color. A torrent of water, loosed.

Tablecloth flung across an empty table. Sit and eat, lie down and sleep. Disowned, misremembered. Today held its breath for a long time under the current. Taught me little or left me what to say.

Today the doorbell's clamor, the wanting and wanting to turn away.

•

A couple of apples coated in wax and an unhappy orange. Today was a little long. A little bruised for my taste.

Yesterday was a city of browning roses. Without water the thorns choke the buds. Or so I was told. Scolded. Yesterday I held in warm arms and fed. Today still slumbering when I woke, its eyes hooded. And the cry of someone's hunger, ungovernable.

Today was children hoarding toys in the supermarket playroom. Let go, one screamed at the other. Arms tore outward like branches scratching the sky. And a distant wave broke over my eyes.

•

A song in hazy water, a deep-down rose languid in the hot. Twined along fences. The song bore words wakeful and mild. I was wrapped in red and granted a feast of clover.

Today the midwife, the tax collector, the father stamping in his button-down. Today twenty methods of sleep for the unquiet.

•

A slice of neon light in a doorway I entered in order to say, I'm hungry,
or, I cannot refuse. And nothing the day is unwilling to give. A dress,
a trundle bed, a plastic bag of food. Yesterday swims in yellow airless
shadows, my arms reaching awkwardly up.

Salt in the rose's eye. I could not sleep so someone spoke for me. Murmurs
in the aisles all crying here. Fell into the nest of rock dust, blood
meal, lake moss, ashes. Now shut up your gaze.

Today wanted my lungs and stomach, my circling animal mind. Today was a
woman whose face I recognized, having lived inside.

•

Nothing brushed or mended or sewed up tight. Today a semblance, something
to be said, expectant. You must eat for us both, I heard her say.

Breathless. Her voice going high and dark, nursing the solstice to the
slow-swinging sea. Oh hush thee my baby the night is behind us. Swinging
down to ease, to ease. From her mouth to my ear, grace.

I have not earned it, I said, though I was famished. Coughing up salt
water.

•

Today bad weather in the lungs, a language more steadfast for its weeping,
a long evening star signaling exile.

To carry the tide, a responsibility, a parcel, to be carried away, to
support or bear, to carry on.

Today a debt to eat or let rot in the cupboard. Yesterday a body growing
distant, earthward. To love is territory and darkness.

Yesterday an unkind surface, common as night pulled over the head.

•

Once I slept inside her and all her thoughts were mine. A habit of pausing
for an idea to offer itself. An unexpected gift, a knock. There, a bent
arm that mimics a plane passing overhead, or a door unhinged.

Hunger is reborn, as is sleep. In the dream I was eating for two. But all
stories fade at the close. Today I am this house's sole occupant, its
hungry embrace. What do you want, I asked the open door. ⁄⁄

YOU TELL ME IT'S THE INSTITUTION: CREATIVE WRITING AND LITERARY HISTORY

KENNETH W. WARREN

I SPENT SIX WEEKS during the summer before my senior year of high school attending a creative writing course called "The Composing Process" at the Phillips Academy Andover Summer Session. It was 1974 and Richard Nixon was being forced from office as a result of the Watergate burglaries and the subsequent cover-up, yet for me the most momentous aspect of that summer was not the nation's political crisis but the idea that I, a skinny black kid from a public high school in Albuquerque, New Mexico, might be on my way to becoming a writer of serious literature. We read *In Our Time* and *Absalom, Absalom!*, among other classic work, and I tried my hand with Hemingwayesque short fiction and imagist-inspired poetry, to the praise of my instructor and to what seemed like the admiration of my classmates. The reading was a revelation, and the fact that some of the pieces I wrote took on, to my eyes, the aura of "real" literature gave me some assurance that I, too, might also some day become a "real" writer. Perfecting artistic craftsmanship felt as important as knowing what was up politically, and that feeling helped me justify my as yet unspoken belief that once I got to college I could treat the sciences and social sciences as barely tolerable nuisances while I pursued matters of real importance on the pages of novels, poetry chapbooks, and anthologies.

In retrospect, the only thing that now seems a little odd about the trajectory I had laid out for myself is that it didn't include any intention to take creative writing courses or to enroll in the creative writing track. There were many reasons for this, but chief among these was my being burdened with a sense of *lack* — the feeling that I lacked the intellectual background and the lived experience to give my efforts the erudition and depth of knowing that I found so compelling in the works I admired. Instead of creative writing, I opted for a History and Literature concentration because, notwithstanding the praise I'd received for my early ventures, I felt I still had to *become* the kind of person who could write real literature. To be sure, I continued to compose poetry along with unfinished drafts of short stories, and I did begin "comping" for *The Advocate*, Harvard's literary magazine, until my diffidence and a sense of isolation derailed me, but I remained convinced that the best writers and the best writing were "unschooled" and that I wasn't missing much by missing formal courses designed for the purpose. The life that would produce the writer was only beginning — or so I thought.

What I had in fact begun was a life that would produce not the novelist or the poet, but the scholar (albeit one with a few published poems here and there and an unpublished novel sitting on his hard drive). Yet in thinking about Mark McGurl's *The Program Era: Postwar Fiction and the Rise of Creative Writing* (Harvard 2009), which takes up — in a way that can't help but impress you with its comprehensiveness — the rise of creative writing programs on college campuses, I can see how my own internal debates about fiction, knowledge, and experience were anticipated, reflected, and shaped by institutional imperatives that almost dictated that someone like me, "having conceived a desire to become that mythical thing, a *writer*" would proceed "as a matter of course to request *application materials*" of one sort or another.

Indeed, even my sense of isolation as a young black writer among what seemed to be an all-white staff at *The Advocate* (a feeling that surprised me because I had spent most of my life comfortably in majority-white settings) might be described as a function of, rather than a critique of, the institution of creative writing as a whole. Race, or racial difference, was an important component of the insider/outsider dynamic that has come to define the project of producing American writers academically. This fact was driven home to me recently as I read Junot Díaz's reflections on his own sense of isolation as a student in Cornell University's MFA program in creative writing in the 1990s. As Díaz recalls, the program was:

> Too white as in Cornell had almost no POC — no people of color — in it. Too white as in the MFA had no faculty of color in the fiction program — like none — and neither the faculty nor the administration saw that lack of color as a big problem. (At least the students are diverse, they told us.) Too white as in my workshop reproduced exactly the dominant culture's blind spots and assumptions around race and racism (and sexism and heteronormativity, etc). In my workshop there was an almost lunatical belief that race was no longer a major social force (it's class!).

In Díaz's retelling, this avalanche of whiteness might have caused him to leave Cornell in the way that I left the offices of the *Advocate* but for his having gotten involved in a Latino student movement on campus that agitated for various changes in Cornell's intellectual and social life. According to Díaz, the movement counted among its "crowning triumphs" the hiring of Helena Maria Viramontes, the program's "first fiction faculty of color." Although Ms. Viramontes did not arrive until after Díaz had graduated from the program, he describes her as "exactly the faculty I had dreamed about during my MFA" — someone who "came out of the tradition of Chicana feminist artists, of women of color artists, the tradition of resistance." He assures us that in her workshops, unlike those he experienced, there would be no pretense that racism and sexism did not structure much of contemporary social interaction.

Yet, in listing the various traditions that produced Viramontes, Díaz does not mention that Viramontes is also part of the very system he attacks in his essay. That is, the writer whom Díaz celebrates as an exemplar of the Chicana feminist tradition is also someone who, not so incidentally, received her MFA in Creative Writing from the University of California at Irvine in 1994. So, if for Díaz, the MFA, writ large, constituted the problem for aspiring writers of color, the MFA was also, ironically, part of the solution. In fact, the idea of the creative writing program as a model seems to have been so deeply ingrained in Díaz's thinking that not only does he hail the arrival of this properly credentialed Chicana writer as the looked-for remedy for his intellectual and artistic malaise, but in the years subsequent to his leaving Cornell he also co-founds Voices of Our Nation (VONA), a workshop for writers of color, hosted by the University of Miami, Coral Gables. The VONA model does not culminate with the MFA credential, but its workshop structure and its presumption that the production of good writing demands bringing aspiring writers into a classroom setting with their creative writing peers supervised by established writers are perfectly consonant with what McGurl has labeled the Program Era. In championing the cause of ostensible "outsiders" to the system, Díaz has done nothing so much as reveal the extent to which his assumptions and practices make him an insider to the story that McGurl tells in *The Program Era*, namely, "the rise of the creative writing program […] as the most important event in postwar American literary history."

The Program Era both reflects and reflects on the very problematic that provides the premise for this "No Crisis" series: the fear that academic literary criticism no longer matters coupled with a counter assertion that literary criticism and history (and possibly even literary theory) continue to speak in vital ways to readers who don't have English PhDs. If a great part of what has generated this fear has been a sense that the nation's intellectual life has retreated into the Academy, with the result that specialization and technical precision have elbowed out the capacity to speak accessibly yet intelligently about literature to an audience of well-educated nonspecialists (presumably the role of what were once truly public intellectuals), McGurl perceptively notes that the status of what we regard as serious literature (literary fiction) has likewise become institutionalized. It finds not only its primary audience but also its economic viability within creative writing programs where the salaries that writers earn as teachers enable them to write and publish highly regarded, if often modestly read, works of literature.

Perhaps the most helpful move that McGurl makes in getting his study off the ground is to instrumentalize rather than embrace the handwringing and defensiveness that usually accompany efforts to assess the role of higher education on the nation's literary and intellectual life and, instead, to note straightforwardly that the dramatic rise in creative programs from a "handful" in the 1940s to more than 350 in 2004 has gone largely unremarked by literary scholars seeking to understand and appreciate serious American fiction in the postwar era. His goal is to turn critiques of this phenomenon into a "non-partisan examination of the *reflexivity* and *systematicity* of postwar American literary production." It's not that McGurl doesn't ultimately take a side on the question of whether or not the institutionalization of fiction writing has had more of a detrimental than a salutary effect on the quality of American literature as a whole — by the end of *The Program Era* he makes it quite clear that to his mind the benefits of this transformation clearly outweigh the deficits. He asks rhetorically:

> Do we not bear daily witness to a surfeit of literary excellence, an embarrassment of riches? Is there not more excellent fiction being produced now than anyone has time to read?
>
> What kind of traitor to the mission of mass higher education would you have to be to think otherwise?

Rather, McGurl reaches his conclusion in such a comprehensive and meticulous way that even if one ultimately disagrees with him — and many readers have — it is impossible not to learn a great deal about postwar American writing from this sweeping study.

McGurl's title, as he tells us in his opening pages, is an allusion to Hugh Kenner's 1971 landmark study of literary modernism, *The Pound Era*, which sought to write literary history in terms of the "dominant individual" as the source of creativity and the center of influence. *The Program Era* does not so much argue for a contrast between the individual and the institution as it describes and analyzes a transformation in which the values associated with the idea of individual modernist genius get incorporated within the dynamics that shape the creative writing program. In McGurl's words it is precisely the "unresolved tension between the 'confinement' of institutionality and the 'freedom' of creativity that gives creative writing instruction its raison d'être as an *institutionalization of anti-institutionality.*"

If *The Pound Era* could be faulted for the narrowness of its gauge in terms of the writers on which it focuses in relation to the authority it claims for modernist poetry of the interwar period, *The Program Era*'s apparently single-minded focus on fiction writing (McGurl apologizes for leaving poetry to the side) in relation to the rise of creative writing programs enables it to encompass an extraordinary number of writers. McGurl's analysis moves with relative ease and insight across a range of authors including Vladimir Nabokov, Thomas Wolfe, Ernest Hemingway, Nella Larsen, William Faulkner, John Barth, Flannery O'Connor, Philip Roth, Ken Kesey, Wallace Stegner, Ishmael Reed, N. Scott Momaday, Arturo Islas, Sandra Cisneros, Ernest Gaines, Raymond Carver, Joyce Carol Oates, Toni Morrison, and Bharati Mukherjee, to name many but by no means all of the writers who get taken up here. And while McGurl's attention is not dispensed equally across this spectrum, what gives the book its singular power is the way that its historical materialist account of the MFA program makes it possible for McGurl to produce illuminating readings of many of the novels he discusses. The effects (and affects) of the program model become manifest in the content and form of the fiction produced in relation to it.

McGurl lays out and diagrams the way that the tensions among the creative writing program's key values — experience (which emphasizes authenticity derived from memory and observation), creativity (which somewhat contradictorily champions giving rein to imagination and fantasy), and craft (which demands acquaintance with literary lore and tradition, along with constant revision and concentration) — map, respectively, onto the Program Era's "pedagogical imperatives" to "write what you know," to "find your voice," and to "show don't tell." The immediate familiarity of these dicta to anyone who's ever fancied writing a story or novel attests to the pervasiveness of creative writing program's influence on how we think about literature.

But McGurl illustrates how the various schools of fiction writing that we tend to see as at odds with one another along the lines that Junot Díaz bemoans in his essay (e.g., the writing of white males vs. the writing of peoples of color) are actually interrelated parts of the same system. Under the god term "autopoetics" — the idea that however important representing and understanding the world outside oneself (i.e., realism) may be within intellectual and literary life, the making, the representing, and the expressing of oneself as an individual, a member of a marginalized minority group, or as a serious writer constitutes the beginning and end of literary practice — writers of apparently very different stripes are perhaps more accurately seen as multiple points on the same indifference curve. The "campus novel and the portrait of the artist are, then, two of the signature genres of the Program Era," but they are merely "symptoms" of the dynamics of the system as a whole.

McGurl provides helpful terms to identify the key formations of the Program Era, including the term "high cultural pluralism," to designate ethnic minority writers like Castillo, Cisneros, or Morrison. The readings he generates are not meant to shore up static taxonomies (he uses Venn diagrams to represent how they relate to one another), but rather to indicate a relationship that Fredric Jameson, in a probing review of *The Program Era*, calls dialectical. So that although McGurl works carefully to identify the distinctive features of these various formations, the more important work here is to show how writers engage, allegorize, and negotiate the same insider/outsider dynamic in relation to their writing, whether that be in the way that the avatar of High Literature and absolute artistic freedom finds herself uneasy at having submitted herself to the systematization of the University, or the ethnic writer bemoans a sense of being marooned in the sea of whiteness that threatened to drown Díaz at Cornell, or the white lower-class writer, à la Raymond Carver, confronts a feeling of dislocation and unpreparedness when cast among the pedigreed set for whom elite college admission seems almost a birthright.

Although the primary affect accompanying each of these figures is that of shame, the story hardly ends there. As indicated by the fact that the style most readily associated with MFA fiction is Carveresque minimalism, the reticence imposed by the shame of the déclassé writer has been readily transmuted into the pride of craft, an eloquent parsimoniousness (in the school of Hemingway) that has shaped the style of legions of MFA graduates. But the power of the MFA to transform shame into artistic possibility has not been limited to the lower-class white writer. For the ethnic writer who initially believes that her experience lies well outside the boundaries of the literary, the MFA becomes, paradoxically, the mechanism by which that which is deemed not fit to be literature becomes its essence. McGurl quotes Sandra Cisneros's reflection:

> It wasn't until Iowa and the Writers' Workshop that I began writing in the voice I now write in, and, perhaps if it hadn't been for Iowa I wouldn't have made the conscious decision to write in this way. It seems crazy, but until Iowa I had never felt my home, family, and neighborhood unique or worthy of writing about.

Alienation produces a sort of psychic repatriation. What one finds in a place far from home are the tools and the authorization to speak for one's aggrieved but resilient people.

So, *pace* Díaz (and not to deny the reality of his felt sense of alienation at Cornell), the writer as POC is hardly an anomaly to the world of the MFA. Rather, in McGurl's words, "Cisneros, like all artists on campus, is the outsider inside, the *inside-outer*, if you will." So, had I only been smart enough or brazen enough (take your pick) to transmute my sense of lack into artistic plenitude, I would now be — well, I would now be in an office like the one I currently occupy, perhaps on the same or a similar college campus, which is to say that in devoting a significant proportion of my scholarship to the study of African-American literature I may have merely performed the scholarly version of Cisneros's move to make her own experience the subject of her literary output.

Either way, if we follow McGurl's line of thinking, we might be inclined to see the proliferation of high ethnic pluralist writers (and the scholars who write about them) as undeniable evidence that American society has gone in the right direction since the 1970s. The growth of mass higher education that has in turn fueled and benefited from the spread of creative writing programs has resulted in a democratization of what we regard as good literature. The stories of Americans of every ethnic and racial background and from up and down the economic ladder have been incorporated into a system that acknowledges and expresses their lives and beliefs and values, resulting in a literary canon that is a more diverse affair than it was 50 years ago. This is indeed cause for celebration.

Yet, however much this diversity might be reflected in the range of texts being published by

CHARLES GAINES
NUMBERS AND TREES V,
LANDSCAPE, #5, 1989
ACRYLIC SHEET, ACRYLIC
PAINT, WATERCOLOR,
SILKSCREEN, PHOTOGRAPH
46 5/8 X 38 5/8"
COURTESY OF THE ARTIST
SUSANNE VIELMETTER LOS
ANGELES PROJECTS; PHOTO:
ROBERT WEDEMEYER

programmed writers, Christopher Findeisen, in a recently published engagement with *The Program Era* in *PMLA*, suggests that institutions of higher education — even the large public ones whose stated mission is to serve the public good — are now more often barriers to, rather than vehicles for, producing equality. Findeisen suggests that this fact has significant implications for how we ought to assess *The Program Era*. The population of college-going students increasingly reflects the economic inequality of the current moment — poorer students (a population disproportionately black and brown but also significantly white) lack the resources and background to become admissible to the colleges and universities where diverse literary curricula have become widely accepted. If stories of their alienation abound on campus, they, as a group, do not.

Certainly *The Program Era*, like my own personal odyssey, attests to the ever-increasing influence of higher education on the cultural and intellectual life of the nation. The benefits for those of us who have become insider/outsiders have been quite considerable: good jobs, social and cultural influence, respect. But if we pull back the lens just a little bit, the true story appears to be one of class consolidation within — rather than the economic democratization of — American society. And for those of us who find it pretty to think that diversifying literary fiction within the institution of the Academy puts us on the side of the angels, this truth may be a hard pill to swallow. *⫸*

If we are completely without direction our minds will tell us the next step to take.

BRIAN TEARE

for five years I wait for pain
to make meaning of my life

   in the emergency room light tilts sidewise on the floor tiled in a grid

but I am only remembering
promises made in childhood

   white the color of waiting the correlative to long duration without event

Book I of *De Imitatione Christi* says
it is good for man to suffer

   the washed cotton of hospital gowns soft as the cognitive fog of illness

the adversity of earthly life
accustomed to seeing illness

   vaguely interested in emergency as a heightened mode of interpretation

from the outside as a parable
for five years I write poems

   at last the needle hits the vein the sudden blush of blood in the test tube

whether I can walk or not
I give my own life the shape

each sense a membrane vulnerable to the way the nurse sharply says *breathe*

lent to it only by watching
myself believe in the benefit

the white of ice water in a Styrofoam cup and a pill in a pleated paper cup

of a suffering so absolute
we should never think it

the mind's response to line and color the same as its response to sounds

necessary in any distress
to have recourse to human

until event punctures duration and a sense of self rushes into the visual field

consolations but I who am
watching never believed it

I am cold and afraid and alone and I have to piss but I've gotten too sick to walk

and I who write this now
no longer believe it is good

on the gurney in the hallway I begin to believe my response to emergency

I no longer believe it is bad
I only believe it is suffering

reveals the metaphysical grammar I will employ for the rest of my life

and it means nothing at all ⟋

WHAT'S LOVE GOT TO DO WITH IT?:
LOVE AND THEFT IN THE 21ST CENTURY

JONATHAN FREEDMAN

I. LOVE AS THEFT

THE LAST TIME I got drunk, many years ago, I was at a conference in LA, a place by its very nature conducive to the lowering of inhibitions. So I walked up to Eric Lott, whom I had known in a friendly way for so many years, to tell him that I had just taught — yet again — *Love and Theft*, and to inform him how enthusiastically my undergraduates, usually a crafty and cynical bunch, had taken to his arguments. But I opined — I only opine when tipsy — that there seemed something missing not only in their reaction but also in the overall reception of the book. "Everyone gets the theft, Eric." I said, "But what about the love? Dude, what's happened to the love?"

True, there's been love aplenty for *Love and Theft* itself — impelling the book well beyond the standard academic thievery as Lott's arguments swam into the mainstream on their way to the shores of the commonplace. Winner of the very first MLA Prize for a First Book, it's also one of those rare academic tomes that has been able to cross over to the public sphere with equal if not greater éclat. And whom among us does not secretly wish for the extra-academic acclaim this book has received: after all, an album by Bob Dylan was named after it, quotation marks placed around the title to mark Dylan's own non-theft of the title (though I doubt Eric has received royalties). Spike Lee includes a shout-out to the book in the credits to his 2000 film *Bamboozled*. And there's a country group that named itself *Love and Theft* — they specialize in songs about gritty ex-alcoholics (as in their current single "Whiskey on My Breath," in which a bestubbled drinker recovers from a binge, shaves, and prepares to face the world sober). As a sign of the proliferating dissemination of Lott's work, the band *Love and Theft* took their name not from the book but from Dylan's album, minus the quotation marks.

Lott's thesis is simple, its implications profound. He asks us to consider why in the 1830s a new form of mass entertainment emerged: blackface minstrel shows, in which (largely) white performers blacked their faces with cork and performed skits, dances, and songs in the personae (largely) of Southern slaves and assorted hangers-on. Pointing to the popularity of these entertainments in the North, most specifically among working-class audiences in New York, Lott anatomizes the social work that gets done through these responses. Their spectatorship, he argues, simultaneously allowed the audience to vent its own class resentment by identifying with the antiauthoritarian, libidinally free-floating figures in front of them, and to feel superior to those figures: two for the price of one.

But the argument moves on from its rich reading of this cultural moment to an engagement with broader cultural phenomena — the use of minstrel show topoi in Harriet Beecher Stowe's *Uncle Tom's Cabin*, for example — and ultimately to an insistent application to the cultural phenomena of the 20th century as well. What, after all, was Norman Mailer's anatomy of the hipster as a "white negro" but an exemplary case of love and theft? Or, literalizing the trope, what was it when Mick Jagger and Keith Richard's record label was accused of trying to copyright their cover of illiterate bluesman Robert Johnson's "Love in Vain" under murky circumstances at best?

There's no doubt that Lott's book both rode the wave of the 1990s zeitgeist and also added to its power. Indeed, part of the genius of the book — and it is a work of genius — is its ability to fuse a generation's worth of excellent Americanist scholarship, literary and otherwise (it's so lovely for an old fogey like me to see a shout-out in the notes to Perry Miller's *Raven and the Whale*) with a remarkable body of discourse that emerged in the late 1980s and early '90s.

Before moving on, let me enumerate some of these. *Love and Theft*'s conceptual foundation is built on the bedrock of one of the late 20th century's most important schools of critical thought: the Birmingham School of Cultural Studies, which, led by guiding spirit Stuart Hall, emphasized the constitutive power of reception, and in so doing opened spaces, even with the most reactionary-seeming of texts, for reckoning unruly or revolutionary audience responses.

An equally important facet of Lott's argument is a new emphasis on whiteness as a racialized category. While theorized in the early 20th century by Du Bois and Fanon, pursued in historical work by Theodore Allen and in legal studies by Ian Haney López — and for that matter apotheosized by comic Martin Mull — this recognition burst into critical and public awareness a year before *Love and Theft* via Toni Morrison's essays *Playing in the Dark*. This more complex understanding of race also entered into labor history largely through the work of David Roediger, whose *Wages of Whiteness* (the title, significantly, quotes Du Bois) appeared in 1991. Equally significant was the idea of "performativity," derived from analytic philosopher J. L. Austin's exploration of the speech act, first as adapted by deconstructionists, then weaponized as a metalinguistic means of undoing fixities of gender and sex in Judith Butler's *Gender Trouble* (1990). Butler's understanding of the performative utterance morphed into a concern with the performance of gender and sex — her book has much to say about drag as a model of both, for example, and that concern percolated broadly in the period before *Love and Theft* appeared, especially as given currency by Jennie Livingston's documentary of the black and latino drag world in *Paris Is Burning* (1992).

There are lots of other influences simmering in Lott's rich stew of a book — Clifford Geertz and Victor Turner on social ritual as theatricality; Eve Sedgwick on homosocial desire; Louis Althusser on subject-formation; Fredric Jameson's *Political Unconscious* on Marxist hermeneutics. I cite all of these for two reasons. The first is to remind us of just how fruitful was the critical moment in which *Love and Theft* was formulated, written, and published, and how fully we literary and cultural scholars are still living on the critical abundance that this moment produced. What allowed it to become so was the breaking down of boundaries both within and between disciplines. Historians, anthropologists, and literary critics met and mingled, as at a gigantic profession-wide cocktail party. Natalie Davis, Stephen Greenblatt, Clifford Geertz, Louis Montrose, Carlo Ginzburg: all these may be said to have been engaging the methods and manner of each other's fields in the pursuit, in Montrose's words, of the history of texts and the textuality of history. (Even Jameson's Marxist hermeneutics enrolled Lacan and Dante in the Frankfurt School.) The work they produced was imaginative, wide-ranging, speculative, polemical, engaged, engaging, and profoundly transformative for all concerned — and for literary critics in particular. Let's face it: as we abandoned our tweed jackets and frowsy skirts and donned our all-black mufti and designer suits, as we took Stanley Fish's advice and traded in our boxy Volvos for elegant Saabs, as we pontificated knowingly about Foucault, Freud, and French feminism, we were, all of a sudden, cool.

Bliss it was to be alive then, and to be young was very heaven. Pure formalism — the dominant tenor of literary training, whether New Critical or deconstructive — was a thing of the past, but formalist methods weren't. To the contrary: they entered into a spicy ménage à trois with history and theory that seemed to promise a genuinely new way of doing criticism of all sorts, one that went variously under the heading (and spawned guidebooks, anthologies, methodological navel-gazing, and the like) of New Historicism, cultural materialism, cultural poetics, the New Pragmatism, and a host of others. The heyday of these was also the heyday of Lott's book, and his work takes full advantage of the opportunities this conjunction opened up.

But — and this is my second point — *Love and Theft* hazarded a different way of integrating the reading, "theory," and historical practice than that on offer in these hegemonic formulations. In retrospect, all of the movements I've named and some I haven't shared a propensity for the hyperbolized totalization, usually expressed, à la structuralism, in terms of a duality — subversion or containment, resistance or hegemony, masculinist or feminist. Even Foucauldians dutifully defined the hypostasized value of power in dualistic terms as being everywhere and nowhere — everywhere precisely because (in another formulation of this discourse, as is the term "discourse") it is nowhere. Lott, by contrast, integrated theory and history and close reading without ignoring the minute as well as brutish facts of power as they got instantiated in the constitutive American rhetoric of race. Because his central thematic is both material and metaphorical, a specific cultural practice that rose, flourished, and foundered and a set of meanings radiating from it, he's able to have the best of both worlds.

True, he doesn't hesitate to build a larger critical-historical edifice out of this encounter. Here, it's a specific field that helps him. New Criticism and especially deconstruction — the backbone of proto-New Historicist reading methods — never really made much of an impact on American literary criticism. Indeed, a kind of old-fashioned commitment to the historical reigned throughout the heyday of Americanists even when inflected by psychoanalytic or other pre-theoretical theoretical methods, as in the greatest work of one of the greatest Americanists, Leslie Fiedler, whose *Love and Death in the American Novel* gives Lott his title and, perhaps, much of his critical perspective on the homoerotic dynamics of the white attachment to black culture. Impulses toward system-building these critics had galore, but Fiedler, no less than F. O. Matthiessen, or Henry Nash Smith, or Ann Douglas, or Leo Marx, genuinely thought that he was constructing an argument about a cultural form that reified historically specific social engagements and material practices. If the theory of mediation in the so-called myth and symbol school was a bit hazy, the practice was exhilarating in its mixture of cultural specifics and extrapolation from them. Indeed, Smith's Virgin Land hypothesis and its feminist extension in Annette Kolodny's *Lay of the Land* continue to be enormously helpful in understanding fights over global warming, ecology, land use and unfettered development; Leo Marx's *Machine in the Garden* is a powerful way of explaining how Silicon Valley high tech presents itself in the guise of 1960s innocence, merging both machine and garden in a kind of creepy high-tech pastoralism — Huck's raft run aground on the corporate campus.

Lott is the latest and one of the best representatives of this tradition: although he reads American culture through one cultural form of many, he makes us see something new not only in his time frame but in the *longue durée* of US culture at large. Indeed, implications of this argument apply, *mutatis mutandis*, to people of our generation, as the Who memorably dubbed us — that is, those of us who grew up white middle-class rebels in the '60s and '70s. Lott's book shows us the less attractive aspects of our adoration of black culture — our joyous dancing to Motown and our furious foot-tapping to jazz and rhythm and blues. If we donned the mask of faux-blackness in order to stage a revolt against the norms of a bourgeois society, it was only to presage the melancholy inevitability that we were all too eager to join it just a few years later, our musical choices intact but now playing on the sound systems of our Chevy Suburban SUVs (or, *pace* Stanley Fish, Volvos).

And, of course, Lott's argument continues to be germane. Blackface in the most literal sense of the word is strikingly long-lived. Writing in 2015, one must inevitably begin with the sorry episode of Rachel Dolezal, the activist and part-time professor who was outed by her awful evangelical family as a white woman despite her passing for a black one. But Dolezal's masquerade, which I read as more pathetic than heinous, is just the tip of the iceberg. Here are a few data points from the vantage point of the last six months or so. Fashion blogger Alexandra Spencer Instagrammed a backyard portrait of herself in whiteface accompanied by artist/all around fabulous person Cheryl Humphreys, done up in black. African-American actress Amandla Stenberg posted a video entitled "Don't Cash Crop My Cornrows" and later, on Instragram, denounced actress? model? celebrity! Kylie Jenner, who had posted pictures of herself with cornrows. Stenberg also critiqued Miley Cyrus for "us[ing] black women as props" while twerking — a dance originating in African culture made part of the hip-hop scene in black New Orleans during the 1990s. And she lambastes Katy Perry for wild stereotyping in her music video *This Is How We Do*.

Curious, I watched Perry's music video, only to discover a pristine illustration of Lott's thesis. On the one hand, it offers a pop art influenced tribute to African-American culture: there are black as well as white dancers, an iconic image of Michael Jordan's famous one-handed facializing dunk, and a portrait of Aretha Franklin with the word "Respect" underneath. But there are watermelons, watermelons everywhere; Katy appearing in cornrows; even a twerking ice cream sundae. Tellingly the song alludes to a 1995 Montell Jordan hit, *This Is How We Do It* — the melody and words are different, but the beat and the bass line are the same. Given that in the original, the ability to do it — to have fun in a cool, elegant way — is located firmly in black LA ("South Central does it like nobody does"), the meaning of Perry's video is clear: this is how *they* do it, and boy, can't we be just like them if we eat a little watermelon and sing a little soul?

White desire to appropriate blackness either as a way out of the most oppressive aspects of whiteness (as is the case with Dolezal) or as a kind of a rebel-without-a-cause fashion statement (as is the case with Kylie and Katy), then, is a dominant feature of our own cultural present, the origins and dynamics of which Lott's book make crystal clear, in the best myth and symbol tradition. The 19th-century tradition Lott charts shifts when updated to contemporary culture, but it's no less rich for that transposition.

But more: he works out of the American studies tradition of radical dissent. Just as Fiedler's work must be read as a gigantic middle-finger salute to the cultural conformity of his moment — the complacent, consensus-worshipping 1950s — so Lott's book has to be read as a meditation on the increasing conservatism of the white working classes in the 1980s. And beyond, to our own hour, when working-class resentment is finding its voice in Donald Trump's racist appeals rather than Bernie Sanders's economic ones. Lott's moment, it is important to remember, was one in which much attention was given to Stanley Greenberg's 1985 study of Michigan's Macomb County Reagan Democrats, of those working-class whites who turned to the Republican Party in the 1980s out of their resentment of people on "welfare" mingled with unrepentant racism. The election of 1988 was won largely by an out-and-out racist appeal by the patrician George Bush, who thrust a convicted black rapist in the face of white America and made the image stick to his hapless opponent. The lessons of these elections were clearly learned by Bill Clinton, whose campaign was in full swing as Lott was finishing a draft of the book. Attuned to the dynamics of the American psyche like no other politician I know, Clinton made currency of the love-and-theft thesis by blowing his saxophone on *The Arsenio Hall Show* like a veteran bluesman (or perhaps the third member of the Belushi/Aykroyd Blues Brothers, itself a Lottean phenomenon) while denouncing rap singer Sister Souljah for the political extremity of her rhetoric. And he turned to the other side of the transaction with his later transmigration, in the words of Toni Morrison no less, into America's "first black president" at the height of the Monica Lewinsky non-scandal.

Blackness and whiteness thus have not only been intertwined with each other but also intertwined with class and — in an important part of his argument — gender: much of working-class masculinity, Lott shows, has been based on the eroticized identification with the black body and a reaction-formation against that impulse. But, as my examples suggest, there's been in recent years an attraction by white women culture-makers to blackness. True, white women sometimes performed in blackface in the latter years of the minstrel show and sporadically thereafter — Shirley Temple, for example. And some white singers have channeled black voices — think of Madeleine Peyroux, who enacts elegant song stylings with a Billie Holiday–tinted voice. Or Grace Halsell: in the wake of John Howard Griffin's racial-masquerade-cum-investigative-journalism *Black Like Me*, she dyed her skin to investigate life in Harlem and the Deep South, with shocking but unsurprising results, reporting numerous instances of careless degradation and even an attempted rape.

But none of these women have assumed the iconic status of Al Jolson or other white men playing black (Ted Danson, I'm thinking of you!). The ease with which Jenner, Perry, and others (Lady Gaga has appeared in blackface on the cover of *V Magazine*, for example, and Madonna may as well have) have accessed blackness as part of their public identities feels different, new: not so much based on an erotics of identification à la Lott as a way to claim transgressive agency for themselves at a moment when transgression no longer seems possible. Whether I'm right or not, these new twists on the old patterns suggest the pervasiveness as well as the continuing power of love as theft — even if it eventuates in pop culture ephemera as transient as twerking ice cream.

II. THEFT AS LOVE

So much for the theft part of the equation. But this still leaves open the question I posed Eric — what about the love? To be sure, love is a complicated emotion: theft, by comparison, is so very simple to describe. Not that the two have no relation. The great analysts of emotion tell us — Proust is by far the most cogent — that love is as full of ambivalence, rage, will-to-power as it is of tenderness, joy, and exaltation; while exalting the lover, it also frequently seeks to dominate, control, or drain the very otherness of the other that inspired the feeling in the first place, operating, in other words, as a species of theft. But is there a more benign, less ferocious way to think about love? After all, tenderness, joy, exaltation are not emotions that we should wish to do without if we want to stay human. And there are many delicious as well as ferocious subtleties, nuances, and outright mysteries to love, to put it mildly. How to affirm — how to even begin to talk about — that side of the equation without falling into the trap of celebrating ethno-racial appropriation?

Lott's book also begins to help us do so. Buried not very far under the critique of racial theft is a privileging of African American expressive culture as a resource in and of itself — in other words, an object worthy of love. Theft, after all, implies that there's something worth stealing, and celebrating this something is the dominant undersong of Lott's analyses — the *objet petit a*, as it were, of his discursive deconstruction of the American psyche. But one can take this argument even further, in ways that complicate as they confirm Lott's basic thesis. Like love itself, the closer one gets to this object — Black expressive culture — the more complex it seems, particularly in relation to white culture. In the last 100 years perhaps, and certainly within the last 50, African-American and white cultures have been tied together in a complex bond of quotation, ironic and not-so-ironic appropriation, larceny across, through, and above the color line. In other words, again like love itself, it's a big, fat, productive mess — one that has been constitutive of as well as shaped by racialized culture-making in the US.

To make this point concrete, let me turn to another moment from the Los Angeles conference with which I began. Before my own talk at that conference, and well before the champagne, I can assure you, I was wandering around listening to music on (this will tell you how long ago this event happened) my iPod. Obsessed, I shared with all around me, including Eric, who sweetly consented to my putting headphones on his ears, my enthusiasm of that moment: Isaac Hayes's rendition of Burt Bacharach's "Walk on By" from his first hit album, *Hot Buttered Soul* (1969). It's a great version of a great song. Preceded by a wholly original Hayes-penned theme played by a cascade of violins accompanied by a guitar, chorus, and Hammond organ, followed by a vamp on electric guitar, Hayes intones in his deep, deep voice Bacharach's song —

> If you see me walking down the street
> And I start to cry each time we meet
> Walk on by, walk on by [...]

— accompanied by a female chorus interjecting "walk on" at periodic intervals. After the next verse, the song proper concludes, but the music continues to — as it were — walk on, as a series of instruments — oboes, flutes, etc. — take up a different vamp, building into an entire orchestra, multiple guitars, and the chorus creating a wall of sound that lasts for a good six minutes, followed by the guitar and organ moving into dialogue with one another, followed by, of all things, a concluding drum solo. After 12:03, the whole shebang is over, and the listener collapses into a state of sonic exhaustion.

We do so because the song brings together so many musical lifeworlds, to invoke a phrase that doubtless sounds better in German. The Hammond organ comes straight out of the black church where Hayes began his musical career at age five. But if Hayes's basso, too, has more than a slight touch of the church choir about it, the electric guitars emerge from white '60s psychedelic rock (as attested to by the abundant use of the late, unlamented wah-wah pedal); the wall of sound, of course, builds on the work of Phil Spector. And the song was written by the great Jewish-American songwriter Burt Bacharach (words by his most accomplished lyricist, Hal David). The song offers an object lesson of the coming together of African-American and white music — to the complication of both.

Before turning to the specifics of Hayes's ethno-racial torquing, a few words about Bacharach's are perhaps relevant here. For black and white were intertwined in Bacharach's oeuvre well before Hayes adapted his music: while he is of course white and Jewish, Bacharach's work bore deep relation to the tradition from which Hayes comes. Initially, white singers wouldn't take his songs, so he wrote for emerging black artists like Jerry Butler, the Shirelles, and Chuck Jackson. Not only was the last named's greatest hit, "Any Day Now," written by Bacharach, he also backed up the singer, playing the distinctive organ riff that begins and punctuates the tune. From a TV show, here's Bacharach playing the organ, dressed as if he's leaving after the performance for the Yale Club:

Their relation is a bit confounding, since the mordents and trills of the organ seem to contrast with the sincerity of Jackson's delivery of the song. It seems a case of uptight white vs. expressive black musical styles, the two brought together as a kind of a metaphysical conceit, as heterogeneous elements yoked together with a certain violence, rather than as a fully integrated unity. But the relation between Bacharach's organ-playing and Jackson's singing is more complex. Not until you hear the opening lick on Jackson's Apollo Theater version of "Any Day Now," played by the tightest of tight horn sections, do you see its family resemblance to the great licks that backed up the likes of James Brown or Wilson Pickett; it's closest in fact to the thrilling, trilling riff backing up the verses of "Papa's Got a Brand New Bag" or "I Got You (I Feel Good)." Bacharach is playing a classic African-American riff even when costumed as a blue-blazered blue blood — a Jew playing Black by passing for a WASP.

This and other collaborations across a still-extant race line, Bacharach claimed, changed his work. "You start working with non-white singers and it's a different tone, there's a soulful thing about it," he told an interviewer. "And that [still] influences what I'm composing and the way I'm working." Nowhere were these influences clearer than in his long collaboration with Dionne Warwick, originally a backup singer on an album he was making with the Drifters whom he singled out and made his muse, as she was entrusted the interpretation of his most difficult songs — which is to say, all of them. Bacharach famously said of her that "her voice had all the delicacy and mystery of sailing ships in bottles," but this misstates the nature of their relationship. Because of Warwick's superb musicianship as well as the flexibility of her instrument, they grew together; he wrote for her, she pushed him. Ken Emerson quotes Bacharach: "The more that I was exposed to [her talent] musically, the more risks, the more chances, I could take." They made each other.

But after offering to their mutual profit definitive versions of much of his work (e.g., "Do You Know the Way to San Jose," "I Say a Little Prayer"), Warwick fell out with Bacharach over what seemed to be petty contractual matters that must have been more personal, then half-heartedly reunited with him much later in her career, a pattern that would look suspicious if it didn't resemble Bacharach's relation with everyone whom he came in contact with — not only his three wives but also his songwriting partner, Hal David. Burt Bacharach — he's a complicated man who no one understands, it seems, even his women.

Bacharach's relations with Black expressive culture extended beyond his collaborations with African-American musicians. His work is also a racial hodgepodge of multiple influences and engagements. Classically trained — he studied with Darius Milhaud — deeply influenced by the jazz tradition — bebop was one of his first loves — and disciplined by the songwriting tradition of Tin Pan Alley and its successors — Bacharach began his career working in the famous popular music incubator the Brill Building, where he, Carole King, Johnny Mercer, and a host of others had offices — his music is double-edged: compulsively melodic, like so many Brill Building products, yet at the same time fiendishly difficult in the manner of Milhaud and bebop alike. Its chord changes are rapid, complex, unexpected; so too are its rhythms. Bacharach is famous for rapid changes in time signatures — while "Walk On By" is set in 4/4 time, the phrases of the song deviate from that pattern, effectively creating measures of 3/4 and 5/4 time. (Try beating out a steady 4/4 beat and saying "walk on by," laying equal stress on each syllable, and you'll see what I mean.) No wonder avant-garde saxophonist John Zorn writes:

> Bacharach's songs explode the expectations of what a popular song is supposed to be. Advanced harmonies and chord changes with unexpected turnarounds and modulations, unusual changing time signatures and rhythmic twists, often in uneven numbers of bars. But he makes it all sound so natural you can't get it out of your head or stop whistling it. Maddeningly complex, sometimes deceptively simple, these are more than just great pop songs: these are deep explorations of the materials of music and should be studied and treasured with as much care and diligence we accord any great works of art.

Far be it for me to argue with Zorn, but it seems to me that his words could apply as well to any of the great jazz artists of the bebop era — and their "explod[ing] the expectations of what a popular song is supposed to be" seems to me what Bacharach learned from bebop. Considered as an ethno-racial transaction, this relation is enormously complex. If Bacharach is inspired by the experiments of these jazz artists, their own "explorations of the materials of music" were not formal exercises; playing with time signatures, adding weird chord changes, interpolating snatches of other songs (shades of sampling!), they entered into contestatory, revisionary relation with a white music that was itself influenced by the jazz and blues pioneers — often in ways that turn the *Love and Theft* paradigm upside down and inside out.

Consider as an example of this the fate of Gershwin's "Summertime," from *Porgy and Bess*, which scholars have definitively identified as a re-rendering of the great spiritual "Sometimes I Feel Like a Motherless Child." (And who needs scholars? Anyone doubting this can listen to Mahalia Jackson's recording of the two back-to-back, seamlessly morphing into one another.) This seems a straightforward case of love as theft; yet making matters more complex, Gershwin is doing some sampling of his own here. In writing "Summertime" he may have also had an old Yiddish lullaby in mind, according to Jack Gottlieb, who goes on to quote a great anecdote from the greatest of all film composers, Bernard Herrmann:

> "Do you think [Summertime] sounds colored?" [Gershwin] asked me. … I said, "What difference does it make? Negro music, Jewish music, they're all quite alike." George said, "I'm still worried. It starts my Porgy and Bess. People may think it sounds too Yiddish."

Amalgamation approaches appropriation, and both yield to self-transformation along the Lottean lines suggested by scholars like Michael Rogin and Jeffrey Melnick, who have argued that Jews like Gershwin took on the mantle of blackness in order to affirm their whiteness. But this is not the end of the story. Like many Gershwin songs, "Summertime" went on to become a jazz standard, indeed, as something of an anthem of the jazz avant-garde of the bebop and post-bop eras. What else can one make of the amazing versions of "Summertime" by (among others) Charlie Parker, Sonny Rollins (including an outstanding duet with Coleman Hawkins), Miles Davis, John Coltrane, Billie Holiday, Ella Fitzgerald, Sarah Vaughan? (I set aside Miles Davis's fantastic recording with Gil Evans's orchestrations, which raises a whole different set of issues.) In these versions, "Summertime" is wholly transformed by the ministrations of jazz improvisation and the extravagancies of arrangement. Its lyrics become occasion for scat singing and, at times, outright mockery (Fitzgerald); its phrasing gets rearranged to emphasize blues intonations (Vaughan); it's put in a raunchy New Orleans–inflected arrangement (Holiday — featuring a truly inspired clarinet solo by Artie Shaw), made the object of a dissonant dialogue (Rollins and Hawkins); turned inside out and upside down and round about in one of John Coltrane's greatest recordings, on what remains for me my favorite of his albums, *My Favorite Things*.

There's an aggressive tenor to this profusion of "Summertimes," as if the largely black jazz tradition is taking back what is rightfully its property. Something in Gershwin's appropriative revisioning of the spiritual seems to have unlocked the revisionary genius of these reappropriators. They resituate his music on their own ground, and in so doing they also acknowledge the basic facts of their own condition. Rootless cosmopolitans, urban sophisticates, musical modernists, whatever one wants to call them, their existential condition was that of alienation; they found themselves utterly cut off from the world that birthed "Sometimes I Feel Like a Motherless Child," much less Gershwin and DuBose Heyward's fictive recreation of that world and its music. But I wonder if in some deep way they don't seek to reapproach both through the mediation of Gershwin's appropriating effort even while, with their increasingly extravagant variations, they demonstrate their distance from it. The path of theft, or in this case countertheft, becomes for them a way of accessing, or reaccessing, love.

We seem to have wandered a bit from Isaac Hayes much less Burt Bacharach, but not really: in fact, I've only begun to unpeel the set of crossings between black and white that generate this version of the song and that persist in it, layered but intertwined. For Hayes is engaged in an act of transformation vis-à-vis the unfolding tradition of soul music as profound as the bop revolution was for jazz. Soul music, broadly defined, begins as a kind of secularization of the gospel tradition by its merger with rhythm and blues in the aftermath of World War II. Particularly in the 1950s and early '60s, black artists like Sam Cooke, Ray Charles, James Brown, Aretha Franklin, the Supremes, and the Temptations brought this music to a new pitch of popularity, with studio "sounds" generated by labels like Motown in Detroit, Stax in Memphis, and Atlantic in New York reticulating the genre in distinct, recognizable contours. Hayes (a completely self-made musical genius who essentially walked into the studio from his day job in a slaughterhouse) worked at Stax as a producer and songwriter — he took the inspiration for the hit he wrote for Sam and Dave, "Hold On, I'm Comin'," it is said, from the words of a musician stuck in the bathroom; and doubtless he saw the writing on the wall for the pure soul tradition in face of the post-Civil Rights era.

For in so many other venues, the period posed black artists a dilemma: an increased racial and political awareness accompanied by a decline in the power of black-only institutions and the concomitant opportunities in the opening of white-only ones to African Americans. Like so many other cultural and social institutions, soul music began to morph in the late 1960s. Motown went mainstream; black soul artists like Aretha Franklin were explicitly marketed to white *and* black audiences (one of my favorite Aretha records, in fact, is her *Live at the Fillmore* album from the *annus mirabilis* of 1971) and continued to record songs by great white songwriters like Bacharach and Brill Building regular Carole King ("Up on the Roof," by the Drifters; "(You Make Me Feel Like) A Natural Woman," sung so magisterially by Aretha) and by white groups like the Beatles (Aretha recorded "Let It Be" in 1970; it is rumored that Paul McCartney originally wrote the song with her in mind). But at the same time, black artists became profoundly engaged with politics as well as the great mainstays of soul music, sex and religion — witness the two great staples of classic soul: Marvin Gaye's great album *What's Going On*, which preceded and in some sense serves as the dialectical twin of his perhaps even greater *Let's Get It On*. Psychedelic and other rock effects made their way into the soul palette from rock 'n' roll even as rock ripped off many of the licks and energies from the soul tradition.

And right at the center of these swirling changes stood Isaac Lee Hayes Jr. As he moved from producer and songwriter to performer, Hayes surprised the world with the mighty effort that was *Hot Buttered Soul*, for which he asked (and received) complete creative control. (Stax was happy to give it to him, since his first album was a failure, and they considered his second a vanity project.) Considered ethno-racially, the album is an interestingly mixed performance, words I use consciously. On the one hand, it begins Hayes's habit of offering elongated versions of standards — the other one on this album is "By the Time I Get to Phoenix" (a song made famous by Glen Campbell but actually written by another great American original, Jimmy Webb), to which Hayes offers a long spoken preamble, adding a prestory to Webb's lyrics — to be followed later in his career by covers/utter transformations of "I'll Never Fall In Love Again," "I Stand Accused," "Never Can Say Goodbye," "The Look of Love," some of them topping 10 minutes in length. But at the same time, and for the first time, he image of overtly sexual black masculinity — shaved head, sunglasses, chains, bare chest: witness the cover of *Hot Buttered Soul* —

At first Hayes hated the nickname, but came to change his mind:

> I had nothing to do with it. I was kicking and screaming all the way. But when I saw the relevance and effect that it had on people, it wasn't a negative thing. It was a healing thing, it was an inspiring thing. It raised the level of black consciousness in the States. People were proud to be black. Black men could finally stand up and be men because here's Black Moses, he's the epitome of black masculinity. Chains that once represented bondage and slavery can now be a sign of power and strength and sexuality and virility.

There's much to be said about the equation of power, strength, sexuality, and virility, not all of it positive (for its problematic apotheosis, see the lyrics for the theme song to *Shaft*, a movie role, incidentally, that he unsuccessfully auditioned for: "the black private dick / That's a sex machine to all the chicks," to which the female chorus responds "I'm talkin; about Shaft/John Shaft...."). But I'd also point to the same habit that runs through so much of the music I've been talking about here: the reappropriation and transvaluation of objects attached to blackness — or more properly the habit of turning objects into symbols, then turning those symbols upside down, so that chains can become a signifier of freedom and baldness a guarantee of virility. (Without getting into the whole black/Jewish thing here, let's just note that the late '60s saw a tug-of-war between the two minorities staged on precisely the ground of who was liberated from what — of whether the Black Moses or the Jewish have a greater claim on the imagination of contemporary culture; here I merely note that this is the pattern of theft/countertheft *in excelsis*.) Love and theft; theft and love: Hayes's oeuvre and self-presentation alike testify to a process of making and remaking in which representations bounce back and forth across the color line, a process in which Hayes remakes himself by lifting Bacharach's happy-sad lover's lament, turning it into a crossover vehicle for himself *and* a way of asserting a newly puissant form of black masculinity.

It's these reverberations we need to have as the backbeat for thinking about Lott's trope as we approach the engagements of our own century. And they keep on keeping on, as the song says, and in more interesting ways than the paths blazed by Kylie, Miley, and Katy. Let me conclude with one final example, which connects Bacharach and Hayes to the politics of our moment and to the history whose nightmares we are not permitted to escape: the hip-hop group Wu-Tang Clan's *I Can't Go to Sleep*, from 2000. For that song continues the process of appropriation and remaking by sampling Hayes's arrangement of Bacharach's "Walk on By." To the austere and impressive tones of Hayes's vamp, rapper RZA describes his inability to gain the peace of slumber as he dwells on (and in) America's spasms of racialized violence:

> I can't go to sleep, I can't shut my eyes
> They shot the father at his mom's building seven times
> They shot Malcolm in the chest, front of his little seeds
> Jesse watched as they shot King on the balcony
> Exported Marcus Garvey cause he tried to spark us
> With the knowledge of ourselves and our forefathers
> Oh Jacqueline, you heard the rifle shots cracklin'
> Her husband's head in her hands, you tried to put it back in

The relation between the words ("I can't sleep") and the music ("Walk on By") suggests the dimensions of his dilemma: if he can neither sleep nor walk away, he's caught in an essential contradiction that leads to paralysis, despair — and ultimately, he implies, drugs, drink, and violence. But who should appear to offer challenge, consolation, warning, but — Isaac Hayes. Hayes arrives costumed as an amalgam of Black Moses and Obi-Wan Kenobi.

So does his basso, featured in a lyrical line that differs from those of the increasingly nervous rapper. Shaking his finger at the sleepless RZA, he offers words of tough transgenerational love.

> Don't kill your brother, learn to love each other
> Don't get mad, cause it ain't that bad
> Look at who you are, you've come too far
> It's in your hands, just be a man,

And after another bout of despair from RZA, the last words of the song belong to Hayes, singing then speaking over his own cascading guitar riff from "Walk on By":

> Don't let the game make you lose your head
> You should be calling the shots instead
> The power is in your hands
> Stop all this crying and be a man

These words enact a generational and experiential conflict in the African-American tradition, one which turns on questions of authority and experience, masculinity and resolve. Bringing in Hayes, however, suggests continuity as well as divergence. For Wu-Tang Clan's use of Hayes mimics Hayes's use of Bacharach: just as Hayes writes his own theme music to resituate "Walk on By," so Wu-Tang Clan reset Hayes's music in their own domain, make him sing his words of caution in their chosen idiom. In both cases the process of love and theft can't be separated from the making and remaking of racial identities, the establishing and breaking down of boundaries, of the cathexes and counter-cathexes that shape intra- as well as interracial structures of feeling.

Theft as love, love as theft: varieties of all of the affective stances they generate are as evident in the stylings of wannabe white women as they are of despairing rappers; in the transactions of Gershwin as in spirituals; in be-bop musical pioners as in Gershwin; in Bacharach as in Dionne Warwick; in Isaac Hayes as in Bacharach; in Wu-Tang Clan as in Isaac Hayes; as, let's face it, me and all of the above. Whatever else we can say about the fate of love and theft in the 21st century, one thing is clear: no matter how hard we try to turn our heads aside, as Americans of any race, we must remain attentive to way that dynamic shaped and continues to shape our cultural experience — and with it our social reality. When it comes to love, theft, and the creative frenzy generated by their interaction, whether good, bad, or ugly, we have to deal: we can't just walk on by. ⬛

ADRIAN PIPER'S CRITICAL INVESTIGATION

TAVIA NYONG'O

ADRIAN PIPER as critic? It seems an unlikely role to grant, even to as multifaceted a person as she. Artist, philosopher, and yogi, yes. But under which of these labels, if not some other, are we to understand her as also contributing to contemporary critical practice? The critic, Terry Eagleton informs us, began in struggle against the absolutist state.[1] The critic contributed to the creation of a bourgeois public sphere within which it would be possible for the rigorous exchange of reason to occur. Today, as in the 18th century, the actually existing public sphere is a torrent of abuses, shock tactics, malicious lies, and horrifying executions. Neoliberal globalization is a crazed horse at furious gallop from which the bourgeoisie — who sought to steer it — has long since been thrown. Within the melee, Adrian Piper keeps her own compass, transforming without being transformed. If there is an oeuvre, it must be in the Idea of Adrian Piper herself, who sheds external appearances with the gentle exfoliant of time. One work of hers, currently on display, consists of glass jars containing her hair and toenail clippings; when it is complete, a final jar will be added with the ashes of the body of the artist herself.

"Everything will be taken away." It is one possible translation of an imperious phrase from an angry king in a parable Jesus tells, punishing a distrustful servant who fails to invest a sum properly. It is also a phrase written in henna on the foreheads of participants in a durational performance by Piper in the summer of 2007 in New York City. Lettered in reverse so as to be readable in mirrors, the participants wore this stigmata/*memento mori* on their faces until it faded. The same message appears repeatedly on two chalkboards — written forward this time — in Piper's contribution to this year's Biennale in Venice. Bart Simpson is nowhere visible, but the piece unmistakably alludes to the miscreant schoolchild made to repeatedly write out a morally improving message on the chalkboard (surely the most Kantian of punishments). You will be changed; you will be dust; everything you have will be taken away. How is one to find any modicum of peace and equanimity — and a sense of personal direction — amongst this inner and outer turmoil?

Conceptual writing has been Piper's métier since early adolescence (diaristic fragments from that age appear in her later adult work, and an early fascination with psychedelia and *Alice in Wonderland* survives in paintings on canvas that have recently resurfaced and been exhibited). Piper is certainly a copious writer, with artist's writings extending to two volumes in print, with more on the way, and another two-volume philosophical treatise on Kant and Hume available for free download from her website. Much of her work — from *Cornered* to her famous *Calling Cards* — can be thought of as language-centered. But she is rarely one for games. A very serious and stern letter posted to her website lists all the various combinations of female, black, and African American that she requests other writers not append to her professional identity as philosopher and artist.[2] The list is astonishing, and a bit irritating. Why bother correcting someone who opts to refer to you as "an artist who happens to be African American and a woman"? "I have earned the right to be called a philosopher and artist," is Piper's response. But perhaps in that earning, in that increase of philosophy and creativity, something has been lost. Everything will be taken away.

As befits the tradition of conceptual art she helped found, the sentence is a fundamental building block of her work. But, like Karl Marx before her, the purpose of her sentences is not to interpret the world, but to change it. She does not provide close readings of things so much as she alters the conditions under which any possible future close reading of those things could occur. Her best work takes a shape similar to the archaic sculpture that Rilke wrote of; it is in its very stillness that it moves you. "You must change your life."[3] It is the case however that her critical function is not addressed to the absolutist state but to you, here, in the "indexical present," as she refers to it in her writings. The indexical present is the locus within which the speaking subject manifests within time and language, hence her sometime resistance to be defined as a "performance artist," with its associated implications of the live presence of the artist. Piper's live presence in her work is rarely necessary for a piece and never sufficient. She has ceased responding to requests for interviews about her work (she will gladly still conduct a seminar for you on yogic or Kantian philosophy) because she has seen that this calls too much attention to her, her private personality, history, motives, and so on. The indexical present — that which binds "I" to "you" as the presupposition to any kind of reference or signification — must rove much more restlessly through the socius, forward and perhaps even backward in time.

For example, consider her most recent catalytic action — her 2013 piece *The Probable Trust Registry: The Rules of the Game #1-3* — which won top honors at this year's Venice Biennale. The piece centers on three sentences that her audience is invited to commit themselves to, by signing a contract with themselves to be deposited in perpetuity at the Adrian Piper Research Archive Foundation in Berlin, where the artist currently resides. On her website, she declares that all interpretations of the work, such as this one, should be considered part of the work. On the day of my visit, I asked a woman facilitating the contract signing which vow was the most popular with the general public. She told me it was "I will always be too expensive to buy," which made sense to me, since of the three it is the one that seems the most self-flattering and least counter to contemporary bourgeois mores. Who wants to think themselves cheap enough to buy, except the very humblest and most grounded among us?

Myself, I wavered between signing the other two — "I will always mean what I say" and "I will always do what I say I am going to do." All three bind the signer in a manner that befits the Kantian rationality to which Piper is committed. In this worldview there is no moral enforcer higher than the rational self, but the price of rational choice is adherence to a code of self-consistency. There are currents of Stoicism and yogic self-discipline in this worldview as well. The presence of that word "always" binds the speaking subject to itself in a manner that scorns the tempting transformations, intoxications, and metamorphoses of the modern flux. The *Probable Trust Registry* (whose name subtly ironizes the earnest commitments it nevertheless archives) invites us to posit our entry into an anonymous collective of beings, each freely existing as means to their own ends, each in their own way seeking truthfulness and consistency in all their actions.

My best guess as to the meaning of this work is that it represents the artist's personal conception of utopia (of course, personal meanings are to be abjured, but I always say what I mean). The Registry is thus both emancipatory and constrictive. Even though Piper is nowhere present in this work of delegated performance, it still conjures up for me an image of the artist as austere, unrelentingly logical sage, descending from her cloud-hidden retreat in Berlin to address us with sincere admonishment, granting us another chance to clean up our act, face up to the truth of our existence, and at last become what only we can choose to be. Is this an artwork for neoliberal times? It seems unkind to saddle Piper with the kind of baggage a critic like Žižek, for example, has weighed upon Zen, the New Age, ethically sourced coffee, and other contemporary self-improvements. For if Žižek is indeed a walking, expectorating caricature of the ego swollen beyond all proportion (something that is not hidden but only made more manifest by the self-mocking, obscene posture of ridicule he frequently retreats to in order to protect against the real dangers of such inflation), Piper is the kind of person who does indeed seem like she could disappear into a jar.

I have overstated Piper the disciplinarian if only to call more attention to what a striking figure she cuts in contemporary culture, with its prudish voyeurism and ethical laxity. How truly unexpected it is that she would win the coveted Golden Lion with so "minimalist" a work. Piper sometimes laments that people miss the humor in her work, which, it is true, is there. But it is also true that she did not come here to be the life of the party. As a young artist in New York City, she once responded to the hip downtown scene at Max's Kansas City by wandering through the club in long gloves, earplugs, and a blindfold. Of this piece, she wrote:

> Max's was an Art Environment, replete with Art Consciousness and Self-Consciousness about Art Consciousness. To even walk into Max's was to be absorbed into the collective Art Self-Conscious Consciousness, either as object or as collaborator. I didn't want to be absorbed as a collaborator, because that would mean having my own consciousness co-opted and modified by that of others: It would mean allowing my consciousness to be influenced by their perceptions of art, and exposing my perceptions of art to their consciousness, and I didn't want that. I have always had a very strong individualistic streak. My solution was to privatize my own consciousness as much as possible, by depriving it of sensory input from that environment; to isolate it from all tactile, aural, and visual feedback.[4]

What Piper describes here as her individualism is also her essentialism, in the philosophical sense of that epithet. It is her essence, her "consciousness," that she seeks to keep apart and unperturbed by her environment (really, our environment, as she cannot find enough ways to disavow it for us). Of course, she understands this particular attempt at becoming-monad to be a failed one — her attempt at withdrawal was read as extroverted aggression, and thus misunderstood; it was reincorporated into the self-consciousness about art consciousness. Distributing roles in her grand strategy to all of us, as she does in the *Probable Trust Registry*, is one answer to this double bind. As art consciousness disseminates into the rest of the world like a perfume floating in the breeze, its becoming indiscernible provides the occasion for each of us signatories to take up our stations in a subtle, social game.

Piper's antagonism toward the social even surfaces in a piece such as *Funk Lessons*, which can be understood as a riposte to Louis Armstrong's famous claim that if you have to ask what jazz is, you'll never know. Defiantly reducing black social dance to a set of instructions any willing and able person can acquire over the course of a single lesson, Piper demystifies "cool" and confounds critics of cultural appropriation. Her conviction that black social dance is a set of procedures like any other is an implicit and explicit critique of the prevailing white habitus of both philosophy and art, which both tend to occupy the position of external and immobile observer of soulful black bodies in motion. Whether constructing herself as a closed plenum ambulating the frenetic disco, or performing as dance instructor — impishly reducing virtuosity to a two-step process of modular and improvised movement — in either case Piper takes aim at a conception of the self as delimited, on the one hand, by its appetites and, on the other, by its cultural identity. Awakening from her dream of going down the rabbit hole, Piper now seeks the proper measure.

Her magnum opus, a defense of Kantian rationalism over Humean empiricism, takes special aim at what she sees as the prevailing Humean conception of human motivation as being grounded in beliefs and desires, and she instead champions a more universal model of the self as outlined in Kant's *Critique of Pure Reason*, which in her view includes but transcends the Humean conception. She thus cuts a striking philosophical profile in a contemporary art discourse so powerfully shaped by our latter-day Humean, Gilles Deleuze. Deleuze never wants to leave the rabbit hole, and many of us would happily join him and Lewis Carroll and the Mad Hatter there for a tea party that never ends. For Piper, neither Deleuzian desiring-production nor the psychoanalytic theory of desire it sought to challenge satisfies the criteria for rationality and motivation that she outlines. This difference is both a problem and a spur to thought for contemporary criticism, which is indebted to psychoanalysis, Marxism, deconstruction, and post-structuralism. If Piper did not come to be the life of the party, she wants nothing to do with your art theory seminar either.

Not only does Piper roll the clocks back to philosophical controversies that were burning in the 18th century, rather than the 20th, a substantive portion of her asceticism can be attributed to her lifelong practice of yoga, bringing her into step with a praxis that has flourished for millennia. Her insistence that her innovations in conceptual art be taken up in relation to her philosophy and yogic practice may suggest, as Uri McMillan has noted in an important new work on her and other contemporary artists, that Piper is a contradictory figure.[5] Certainly, her creative and critical process display an uncompromising independence of thinking, a form of life that the *Probable Trust Inventory* offers to extend to any who would accept it. Indeed, part of the appeal of the inventory — an appeal it shares with Yoko Ono's *Promise* pieces, or Shelley Jackson's "novel" *Skin* — is the virtual collectivity it projects into the indefinite future. Something short of the rational telos that is a bit simplistically attributed to Enlightenment figures such as Kant, the probability of trust nonetheless constitutes a future that resists its reduction, under contemporary capitalism, to financial derivatives, or, under a Deleuzian philosophy of immanence, to open-ended becoming.

As I mentioned, Piper has recently announced that she will stop commenting upon her artwork, because the net effect of her writing about it, she fears, has been to exacerbate the tendency for critics to read it autobiographically rather than on its own terms. Two of her most famous works (*Calling Cards* and *Cornered*) begin with the statement, "I am black," but she now asks that her work not be interpreted as that of a "black female artist," and has officially "retired" from blackness in order to enter into a gray period. What are we to make of her consistent demurrals from both personal and collective identity? Is it a kind of vanishing act, where the elements that once so clearly delineated her work disappear, one by one, until we are left with just her ironical Cheshire grin?

A recent series of photos, also entitled *Everything Will Be Taken Away*, includes black-and-white snapshot photos of people smiling for the camera, with their eyes (and therefore their identities) scratched out. Philosophy may yet save us from surveillance and our ever-expanding data doubles.

Another work places a bright red target around a faint grayscale image of Trayvon Martin, floating above text that asks us to "Imagine what it was like to be me." There are a number of ways to receive this portrait of Martin, the teenager tragically slain by a Florida vigilante, a human being whose murder went unpunished and ignited the Black Lives Matter movement. This piece hardly seems the work of an artist who has abandoned her critique of racism even as she rejects the routinized patterns through which race is habitually dealt with in public life. If mortality now seems to preoccupy the artist's work in a new way, it is nonetheless a facet we might have chosen to see all along. In Stoic tradition (one possible affinity with Deleuze), Piper's work conjures the specter of impending death not in order to paralyze us with anxiety, but to free us to live more fully in the here and now, in "the indexical present."

The challenge she models for us, her critical instigation, is to live in this present experimentally, a challenge in unexpected accord with the Spinozist-Deleuzian ethics that Piper, as philosopher, may not personally champion, but that Piper, as artist, opens a new door onto. ⁄⁄

ENDNOTES

1. Terry Eagleton, *The Function of Criticism*. (London and New York, Verso: 2006).
2. http://www.adrianpiper.com/dear_editor.shtml
3. Rilke, *Collected Poetry*.
4. Adrian Piper, *Out of Order, Out of Sight: Selected Writings in Meta-Art*, 1968-1992, p. 27.
5. Uri McMillan, *Embodied Avatars*. NYU Press, 2015.

FRANK BENSON
HUMAN STATUE (JESSIE), 2011
BRONZE, MARBLE; 79 1/4 X 12 1/2 X 20"
COURTESY OF THE ARTIST AND ANDREW KREPS GALLERY, NEW YORK

NO, CRISIS

EVAN CALDER WILLIAMS

Be attentive to the voices of the oppressed, the slaves who possess the key knowledge,
and be patient for the most opportune moment for slitting the tyrants' throats.
— *Chris Chitty*

1.

WERE I STILL invested in the weird pathos of being deep into deconstruction a generation too late, I would probably ask for the red slash between "No" and "Crisis" in the logo originally published with this series to be rotated 45 degrees clockwise and moved left a bit, leaving the "No" struck-through and under erasure. Likely for the better, I now find such gestures cloying. Still, a sense of unease with this series' framing has lingered since I was asked to contribute, one I'm unsure of how to mark in writing. That unease doesn't come from any opposition to celebrating incisive and necessary criticism that deserves a first, second, or nth look. It emerges instead from my suspicion of any framework that structures the continued production of such thought and texts as if they happen in spite of austerity. As if the persistence of the former might obviate the severity of the latter, accidentally proving, in answer to the clarion calls of a thousand regents, that we can indeed tighten our belts, narrow our gaze, and plow ahead because, they remind us, we don't do it for the money anyway.

I hope this criticism gets taken close to how it's meant — as the start of a dialogue, as taking something seriously enough to engage with it — rather than as merely pissing the pool. Because it ultimately concerns a problem against which we've been butting our heads for years but which never seems to go away. Simply enough, how to understand a relation between crisis and criticism? In the series' introduction, one version of that relation appears, however obliquely, and it does so in two distinct modes worth calling into doubt.

First: "It is hard to make a living in criticism these days, yet there are some of us who can hardly imagine living without it." I don't disagree with either clause. Real critique, rare thing that it is, usually pays dreck, in no small part because it threatens systems of valuation. And indeed, I can't much imagine a life separate from trying to articulate that critique, even though it only sometimes takes a shape called criticism. It's the "yet" that troubles me, because it risks confirming a structure already mobilized in this moment, within universities and far beyond: that one will be asked to soldier on and ultimately comply because one cares, because one loves it, rather than because one is paid. Historical record is unfortunately clear about the infinite quantities of bullshit, abuse, and humiliation that people put up with — or, when they have the means/capital, violently displace onto others further down the hierarchical steps that end at social death — in order to get paid and get by. And that record is equally clear about the ways that such ordeals are often excused by reference to love or duty, be it monogamous or national. The problem with that "yet" is that it can too easily be tuned otherwise to do this work of naturalizing and mitigating. As if to say, yes, crisis happens, yet criticism is what we love to do and who we are at our best, so we find a way to keep the fires burning when the power cuts out.

Moreover, when we say, however correctly, that people find a way to write necessary criticism during crisis, we have to be extremely lucid about the enormous differences contained in that phrase — especially when a lot of people just can't find a way. For instance: all the other entries in the "No Crisis" series focus on works of criticism written not just by living professors but tenured full professors.[1] I don't doubt that most, if not all, of those professors have found their places of work and intellectual communities under attack in a number of frustrating and disturbing ways. All the same, for them to write criticism during a crisis describes a situation where no matter how toxic the mood, they can remain comparatively secure in continuing to be paid to do so — and to continue as such.

What doesn't continue, though? Who doesn't get supported enough to even start? Not because these have been crisis years within the humanities, and, hence, within criticism, but because these have been crisis years for the global north and, hence, for its universities and their labor? If we want to take account of whether "the art of criticism is flourishing" in such years, we have to recognize that the tenured professor is hardly the primary figure with which to do so, let alone one that crisis has made especially active use of to restructure its terrain. That would be the adjunct, the freelancer, the thinkpiecer, or, in austerity's grammar of hyphenation, the cleaner-writer, baker-critic, debtor-dealer-scholar, nurse-theorist, and on from there, in countless permutations of predicates. The fact that many of my favorite thinkers and writers inhabit such positions is no accident, as their thought moves through spheres of experience that too many forms of scholarship are loath to handle. But they're always stalked by another situation, the one where you have to drop the -writer or -critic portion because you cannot make it hang together and must indeed learn to imagine how to live without it. The crisis of criticism, in other words, won't show itself in the quality of the written. It's in what no longer gets written, in what never gets written in the first place.[2]

---

1. A note: after I wrote this, I noticed that a new addition didn't follow the pattern, as it concerned a dead writer (Vilém Flusser) who was a professor among other things, rather than a career academic. The author of the piece is Kenneth Goldsmith, however, which I can't let pass unnoticed. The ground has been plenty covered, but still, one has to note: his unwillingness to seriously address the extensive criticisms of his performance at Brown this March; his evident refusal to consider saying either *yes, actually, that performance was racist* (as the performance was) or simply, *that was a terrible, terrible idea*; perhaps above all, his apparent assumption, whether convenient side-step or sincere, that the anger behind the critiques was a sign that his critics felt "uncomfortable" or had misunderstood something about conceptual poetics, rather than an all-too-clear recognition of a well-worn operation that disavows any complicity with histories of anti-blackness under the sign of knowing appropriation. All of which is to say that unlike the other entries in this series, I can't take seriously any ideas he might offer about a relation of crisis and criticism.

2. Anne Boyer's recent and necessary book *Garments Against Women* has a remarkable discussion of "not writing." It is excerpted at *Bookforum*, but I recommend getting the book as highly as I recommend all of her writing.

The fact remains that for all the disarray of the humanities and for all the compelling work that happens online or in small publications and new presses, most criticism — including my writing, too; including this essay — still takes place in a zone of cultural production materially predicated on a stable university salary. Most academic journals, for instance, pay literally nothing for essays, with the expectation that the author receives or will receive that salary, and, hence, that her free labor helps solidify or advance her position. Yet it's a salary that I, like a lot of the writers and critics I know, haven't had, a decision largely made for us by the logic of the times. Without that salary, how does one do criticism? Perpetual adjunct work is so stressful and poorly paid that it leaves scant time for writing, let alone extensive research. If you try to make a go of it as a critic further from the university, you navigate between the Scylla of the think piece — a.k.a. an essay that knows it shouldn't exist, and not in some Maurice Blanchot "writing the impossible" mode — and the Charybdis of genuinely interesting publications who sadly can only afford a nominal fee at this time, but we hope that you'll …[3]

In short, you can only do it for love for so long, and that time comes a lot quicker when you lack job security or a job to start. A question of how to write criticism is, in this sense, a question absolutely inseparable from how to critique, from how to resist the most fundamental mechanisms of social domination. Those are the mechanisms that determine who gets to enjoy the relative and anticipatory comfort of a safety net, whether woven of tenure or white privilege, and whose struggles to write and live involve a bitter, fraught sense of precarity."[4] Austerity measures may be imposed generally, but cuts never fall on some uniform body of the nation, the populace. They go deepest into those already expected to bear the brunt of quotidian social violence.

The second thread I'll pull on comes in here: "we hope to show that the art of criticism is flourishing, rich with intellectual power and sustaining beauty, in hard times." In this schematic, hard times are something to be weathered like a winter, lean years in which we take sustenance in thought that flourishes in spite of everything. It's hardly a unique sentiment. One can find the trope in Alain Badiou, for instance, albeit in a more agricultural-meets-partisan register: "philosophy is like the attic where, in difficult times, one accumulates resources, lines up tools, and sharpens knives." There's also something of an older sense of the word "crisis" at work too, coming from a medical designation (the krisis) of an illness's turning point, like a fever's peak, where the already-dire becomes starkly binary: the fever breaks, or the fevered dies. Criticism, in that version, would be the life-giving broth that sees us through, or, conversely, the spiritual reminder of beauty and a vita intellectualis worth living — a model of faith, say — that won't bow under the travails of flesh. Crisis and criticism are set against each other, but not in the sense of a pharmacological interaction or cure. One weakens us, one sustains us, each with designs on the patient in question, but never the two should meet, ships in the night of a single life.

However, I'm struck by how among the best theorists, critics, writers, artists, and organizers I know, the operative relation between crisis and criticism is nearly the opposite. Crisis isn't something

---

3. Flight into that great unregulated market known as the art world is hardly more promising. Offers to give talks or write catalog essays are often paid decently but not enough to plausibly stitch together a living. (The situation is markedly worse for those involved as artists: in an echo of the academic publication as verification for tenure-advance, many of the most famous museums pay artists nothing whatsoever, including for solo exhibitions, because, after all, they are giving them "free publicity" to be hypothetically capitalized upon in the open market.)

4. In *The Undercommons: Fugitive Planning & Black Study*, Stefano Harney and Fred Moten argue that, "the only relationship one can have with the university is a criminal one." In their text, the "only" at hand is largely a tactical injunction for the "subversive intellectual" to "go into the university and steal what one can." It also increasingly seems to plainly describe the situation available to most who might be critics, theorists, or historians, a relationship that comes under the sign of either *hustling* or *no relationship at all*, having left it fully behind. Harney, Stefano and Moten, Fred.

one stoically endures. It is the point of departure for the work of critique, an injunction to read differently. To write through crisis means grappling with how it throws us into disarray, scrambling and reorganizing our daily priorities, but it also clarifies the situation we've been in for years, bringing into relief a fundamental cartography of quotidian circuits — like prison <—> university — that can fly under the radar in easier times. In crisis, the stakes feel higher, and we, too, start to feel indissociably like a we, however briefly. (The fact that the majority of those who think this way are communists is not, and could not be, incidental.)

I start with this gesture of criticizing my hosts — never invite a vampire … — in part because it seems something that should be raised. But in larger part, it's because this essay concerns Chris Chitty, one of those rare thinkers in question. Chris and I met in Santa Cruz, where we were both doing PhDs, though it's perhaps more true to say that we met in an international context of organizing in the past decade: talking, arguing, and laughing in meetings, marches, parties, and cramped occupations. Chris wrote once that Foucault's project and method involves asking, "whether there can be a kind of speech with an alternate relation to truth, speech that is engaged in the struggle and no less committed to truth." It's an old goal and one that never gets old, insofar as the answer is surely yes, there can be, and there must be, yet it will always be threatened by everything arrayed against it. It has to be sustained, not by retreating to the attic, but by insisting anew that speech learn to listen and take its cues from struggles, rather than demand that struggles follow the dictates of speech.

In April 2015, we lost Chris, suddenly and atrociously, and, in him, one who understood this in all its difficulty.

2.

When Foucault starts his 1975–1976 lectures at the Collège de France, lectures Chris knew as well as anyone, he opens with an introduction not to the themes of the year — social war and race struggle, biopower, the birth of the dialectic, and on from there — but to why he gives these lectures. He insists that what he's doing is not teaching, especially not when faced with a lecture hall so packed he tried moving the lectures to early morning to thin the crowd. No, Foucault claims that he is offering the chance for his research to be held accountable, to have his ideas used as those present and elsewhere felt necessary. The gesture strikes me as important, avoiding both proprietary mastery and the false humility of acting like he had nothing special to offer. As he says, "word always gets out" — the ideas will circulate, with futures beyond his control and use of them, singularly compelling as that use was.

Writing about Foucault's earlier 1971 lectures, Chris notes: "If it's hard not to hear artful references to his impending death in some of the final lectures at the Collège in 1984, it's harder not to feel a deeper sense of loss with these lectures, of which there are no recordings, only notes." Losing Chris puts us in a similar position. We are left with essays, talks, remembered conversations, and notes, all marked by his brilliance and originality. But the picture is incomplete, a partial mosaic of his critical project's full sweep. And yes, word always gets out, but sometimes it needs a push, especially from those for whom the thought matters. I can't claim to know what Chris would want to have happen with his work, and I won't pretend to synthesize, steward, or even summarize it. Instead, all I can do is write an attempt to come to grips with what I think was and is so necessary about it.

News of his death reached me in the middle of the night in Copenhagen, three days before I was due to speak on a panel with him in New York. The next day, walking through a sunny park and wanting to spit in the face of literally anything that smiled, a single thought looped through my head: that beyond Chris being a friend and a comrade whom I'd missed since I left California, I also literally learned the meaning of comrade from him. How it came from the Spanish camarada, the French camarade, from roommate, sure, but also how this was literal and physical. How it came from the real sharing of a space together, bound to the bonds formed by men who didn't have security or wealth or private homes and so bedded down in the same small and rented rooms, who were friends and strangers, who fucked or didn't.

This seems a keystone of Chris's queer history that doesn't begin with, or ever settle into, the clarity of an identity. Instead, in his work, the categories of intimacy and the blurry bonds of friendship, as well as society in full and its possible dissolution, are never given. They are always produced. He asks: what happened in the bedroom, the bathroom, the kitchen, behind the barricade, down the alley, within the occupation, in the commune? How were these sites and their activities both real and concepts, both practices and discourses? How were they mobilized in the processes of historical transformation, made into categories, and redeployed? How did they become causes for incarceration or rebellion, entangled in what Chris calls "the functional unity of the forms of appearance of power," whether as support or crack? And what can happen: what are the contours of the possible, not in flight from these spaces but through them?

The possible range of this sort of inquiry can be seen in a single object, a table around which to gather. In the first chapter of his dissertation, titled "Homoeroticism and the Mediterranean World," a table stands at the very beginning, forming the point of historical departure: in Crete's communal mess halls of men, which Aristotle writes, in the Politics, "encouraged sexual relations between men" through "a system of common meals, which the Spartans, in former times, used to call andria."[5] At the end of this chapter, we find ourselves at another table: that of Caravaggio's Cardsharps, a painting whose triangulated "sweetness and fraud" Chris reads for the smallest signs — the dirt under the fingernails of one of the boys, the "delicate (and, no doubt, expensive) needlework," the threadbare gloves of the man — that sketch the trails of tremendous historical shifts, a transformation of the contested Florentine sphere of sex between men.

It's the kind of reading that shares its answer with a question that haunted the whole of Aby Warburg's — and later, Harun Farocki's — research: how do we see the motion of history in a still image? Warburg's answer remained consistent: We see such motion because no image is ever alone. It is always in a sequence, and a genealogy means reading the world as montage. So too for Chris — and so the table will appear again, never meaning the same thing but with enough rhyme to open up a chain of reading across time and social situations. In its third appearance, it's the table at the center of industrializing capitalism's transformed domestic sphere, a product of that process of breaking feudal form and its specific relation of family and property. In this situation, the table must, as Chris writes, "buttress the new social form, as the household was transformed into a center of industrious activity and consumption."

Triangulating these three tables, we can glimpse something of the scope of his project and its capacity to range across and through instances. Just what is that project? In a basic way, it is to develop a material genealogy of homosexuality — and of heterosexuality, too, or what he calls "heteroeroticism," a sexual formation in trajectory — as both practice and concept. More precisely,

---

5. Chris's translation.

I'd say it is to construct a rigorous and ranging account of male homosexuality, a history both of actual sex between men and of how a notion of that activity — as what could be abstracted into a category, an identity, a felony, a crisis — gets produced through long processes that fold in a huge array of elements, operations, and sites, from wharves to poetry, rent to war, urinals to tribunals. Yet it also concerns, in a crucial reversal, how what he once referred to me as a "specter of buggery" can itself produce a certain mode of the political. That specter could spur geopolitical transformations that exceed the seeming purview of conventional histories of homosexuality, and it functioned as a knot of care and moral panic around which social space was formed, fought, and defended.

This sense of homosexuality as at once produced and productive is a crucial reversal at work throughout his research, and I think it reveals how genuinely he followed Foucault in not just content but method as well. For too many who "work on Foucault," that work just means cherry-picking terminology without any sense of the method that generated it. In Chris's words:

> Since his death, the intellectual portrait of Foucault has been drawn by interpreters invested either in making his thought more palatable to liberal quietism — the "resistance is everywhere; all resistance is futile" Foucault — or in a cottage industry that has mined his work for fashionable academic buzz words (panopticism, biopolitics, governmentality, normativity, etc.).

Chris, however, worked in the opposite direction, drawing out a version of Foucault crucially attuned to the forms of research needed for active intervention in times of both crisis and seeming peace. In Foucault, he saw "genealogy's ability to juxtapose radically different conjunctures" to not only cut across a range of those conjunctures but also to articulate what he called, following Foucault in a stunning article and translation for Viewpoint, the "mesh of power" that sustains and reaffirms the texture of social normalcy. In his own words, from the Viewpoint essay:

> The oppressed, Foucault argues, also make use of an immense "network of power." They are not passive victims of a historical process; in fact, power is historically contingent. The resistance of the oppressed has shaped the present organization of power. Revolution, according to this view, is a rare bird indeed.

The strength of this approach, one which is not just Foucault's but Chris's too, doesn't lie only in its insistence that power is multidirectional. It's also based in how it permits a crucial reading of class dynamics itself, one not restricted to interpretation via periods of historical accumulation (as potentially suggested by the broadly Giovanni Arrighi-esque schema through which Chris periodizes). Instead, it offers an angle of approach onto how social form continually works through, not on. Social control's "distended organizational calculus," in Hortense Spiller's words, makes vectors, not victims, we might say, and the work of revolt has neither recourse nor exodus to any structure wholly of its making, let alone a prelapsarian commons, transhistorical species essence, or human community (the notorious, if slippery, Gemeinwesen found in Marx). It must instead make use of the very discursive, circulatory, and spatial patterns that its prior resistance helped form and which now array against it, comprising the weave of society's flexible and homeostatic power.[6]

In this regard, the comparison between Foucault and E. P. Thompson made by Colin Jones and Roy Porter seems relevant to the particular way that Chris picked up on and extended Foucault's method, given the dual emphases on how class is made, not discovered, and on how a loose aggregation of disparate behaviors become a category of condemnation, such as homosexual or witch, primarily in order to veil even larger processes of accumulation and upheaval. So while Chris's thought shares more obvious overlaps with queer militant theorists, like Guy Hocquenghem and Mario Mieli (and involves compelling and almost classical echoes of attention to minor details of rhetoric and text, reminding me of Hans Blumenberg), I've come to see in his work the same spirit of inquiry into social formation and rebellion that marks the work of Silvia Federici and Peter Linebaugh. As in their thought, the task of research is to take history apart at the seams, inverting what could appear as constants, or at least as methodological points of departure — like the queer in queer history — and reveal them to be a messy index of the discrete instances of insurrection and punishment yoked together by that term.

That's the gesture with which Chris's ambitious project begins: not only with the ancient Mediterranean sphere and that first table (the Cretan andria), but also with a sense of how a history of homosexuality drags a number of other crucial social forms into uncomfortable light. One of those is the relation between the communal and the military, a proximity that persists to our own days — think the reversibility of the barricade, for instance — and which in ancient Greek formations forged a particularly strict bond in terms of sex between men (part of that Grecian "martial type"). His crucial turn, however, is a more expansive move, grounding the martial type's civic and erotic construction on the economic foundation underwriting it. Specifically, on the utterly fundamental role of both slavery and gendered domestic work for the kind of transformations that were to enable the very notion of a Greek citizen, and with it, I'd argue, the opposition of theory and praxis that still haunts discussions of crisis and critique.

Reading Chris's discussion of this term sent me back to Aristotle and the Politics, where I found the observation confirmed, both in content and the structure of the text itself. Consider, for instance, the progression of Aristotle's argument that claims to consider the state from the ground up (because "a composite has to be analyzed until we reach things that in composite, since these are the smallest parts of the whole"). It begins with two binaries that function as those first principles, the state's barest elements. Each consists of "those who cannot exist without each other [and] necessarily form a couple": "female and male" (who "do so for the sake of procreation") and "natural ruler and what is ruled," or master and slave: "For if something is capable of rational foresight, it is a natural ruler and master, whereas whatever can use its body to labor is ruled and is a natural slave." Immediately after, however, the threat of category error rears its head, as the question is posed as to the "natural distinction [...] between what is female and what is servile." The answer given is that nature "produces nothing skimpily, but instead makes a single thing for a single task." So follows its allocation of "natural poiesis" (reproduction) and household management (economics) for women,

6. This approach to thinking power has become central to my work as well, albeit from a different source: from my translations of and work on Italian postwar communist theory, in particular the militant sociologist Romano Alquati, who spoke of postwar labor management and its spatial distribution as a *gabbia flessibile*, a "flexible prison." More broadly, I'd say that a heterodox version of workerism – one certainly not centered on the specificity of waged work but still attentive to the dynamics Tronti's "Copernican inversion" – forms a significant element of the thinking of a number of us coming from Santa Cruz, seen in varied forms like an interest in communist historiography to histories of "workers' inquiry."

praxis for slaves (as ktêmata, or property that lets one carry out action), and theory for male citizens.[7]

In this regard, Chris's return to Greek origins doesn't just retread the ground that Foucault, and many others, have crossed. It also reads a tense nexus of civil society itself in the constantly mutating figure of homosexuality. It's what lets us better see how a triangulation of women, slaves, and men (as citizens) becomes and remains a necessary structure on which to erect a notion of citizenship and, with it, a "productive" public sphere — one that capitalism's requisite triad of home, colony, and factory will later amply mobilize in its own way. The Greek formation especially serves as the point of contact and departure for one of the central topics of Chris's project, a reading of the "Mediterranean model of homosexuality" that he sees as predominant from the 12th to the 17th centuries, articulated especially through Florentine history. Reading across legal code, literature, political theory, and labor formation, he argues for the emergence of an "economic type" of homosexuality, as "cultures of sodomy" and "merchant-dominated social formations" came to be seen as necessarily associated and became actually connected through the spatial and discursive sites of the city, the market, and all the outskirts, alleys, docks, and communal zones that formed both their shadows and functional points of circulation. In particular, his project comes to detail how the forms and hierarchies of labor at work in those sites produce a novel relation of "sexual freedom and constraint," resulting in a sexual culture able to a) libidinally capitalize on such labor divisions and b) pose them in a classical republican framework where they are available for political use, far from an opposition of public and private that will dominate bourgeois sexuality. The politics of that, however, were not only, let alone primarily, exercised in a theater of calumny, revenge, or getting one's opponent out of the way. They also functioned as a form of seizing assets and raising revenue from rich and poor alike. Similar to Federici's understanding of the persecution of witches as indissociable from processes of primitive accumulation, Chris reads the history of Italian sodomy law to discern how the penalties functioned as an extra-market accumulation via fines, one that could be pushed too far, as in Venice, whose draconian fees encouraged sailors to avoid the Ufficiali di notte and find laxer ports in which to work and enjoy themselves.

This account and its readings deserve far more space and time than I can give here.[8] Yet perhaps the element of his thinking that most captivated me, and certainly the one we talked of the most, was how all of these dynamics moved through, and became crystallized in, social space, a theme central to other thinkers like Kristin Ross, Sharad Chari, and Giuliana Bruno, from whose texts I've learned a lot. Not that Chris and I agreed on spatial matters, particularly when it came to deciding whether spaces temporarily snatched from normal use or disconnected from markets constituted real breaks from those structures of value and power.[9] All the same, we agreed on two fundamental points. First, we cannot write histories inattentive to the real force of mass affects, in particular creeping panics over social transformation, whether that means white privilege nervously

---

7. It's fitting that "barbarians" first appear in *Politics* in this context, as those who don't draw adequate divisions between women and slaves, because "they do not have anything that naturally rules[…] their community consists of a male and a female slave," and hence, Grecian domination over them is, of course, not just excusable but morally necessary.

8. And where it moves from Florence is equally compelling, with the outpacing of the Italian mode by an "Atlantic" mode of homosexuality in the sixteenth and seventieth centuries that involved complicated set of transformations: a nostalgic late Renaissance "rediscovery" of the ancient form (the homoerotic "essence"); a new "geographically coextensive social formation" with an attendant erotics of circulation; a "transitional world" of European colonizing encounters with, and decimation of, indigenous populations; a complex reading of those comradely boarding rooms and the attempted moral hygienics of public toilets; and the emergence of a notion of "taste against nature" (*le gout anti-nature*) which came to be associated equally with "elite boarding schools" and "primitive societies."

9. This primarily involved a (mostly) good-natured ongoing debate over Burning Man. He described it to me as opening a zone of play and duration beyond the market. I think that given the $390 ticket cost, that's like buying all your groceries for the week on Sunday and then acting like you eat beyond the value-form Monday to Saturday …

watching its social power ever-so-slightly diminish or a petite bourgeoisie alarmed by the coherence and strength of proletarian communities. Yet this doesn't mean entering into classical ideology critique and truffling for symptoms. It's rather to see how those who aim to be architects of society, whether fascists, neocons, or liberals, have historically capitalized on this in extremely practical and technically sophisticated ways, no matter how vague their rhetorics of mythic ethno-nationalism and pseudoscience. Fundamentally, they work in order to effect changes whose aims are not to ameliorate anxiety but eradicate dissidence. In a book I can't recommend highly enough, *Anarchism and the City: Revolution and Counter-Revolution in Barcelona, 1898-1937*, Chris Ealham writes of the Spanish situation prior to the Civil War and how,

> For the 'men of order' (gent d'ordre) among the bourgeoisie, the moral panics were a guide to repressive action: they profiled the 'danger' represented by 'recalcitrant' and 'diseased' groups (hence the positivist concern with classifying, cleansing and civilising), which had to be excluded from the full rights of citizenship and isolated from 'healthy' and 'respectable' individuals. They were also a justification for closing off the nascent proletarian public sphere, creating a moral and political climate that legitimated the extension of state power on the streets and the establishment of a new system of bureaucratic surveillance to regulate civil society.

The strength of Ealham's analysis in that book, one visible in Chris's research as well, is its attention to what he calls "spatial militarism" and how it requires we grasp the ceaseless interchanges between two senses of police. There are the productions of a managerial and sanitary cordon, as with the work of the "medical police" of 18th-century Europe, that served to subdivide populations. However, this remains the companion of a concrete and extensive policing of lived space itself, from literal cops forming neo-centurion riot shield formations to the less obvious forms of cordon sanitaire, like the subject of one of Chris's talks, the barriers between urinals intended to make sure that men do not become comrades, so to speak. Even as the two must maintain an appearance of separation, allowing the image of police as objectively and apolitically justified, they maintain an actual mutual dependence, taking alternate turns in plain view without ever ceding ground to what threatens them.

This gets to the heart of the other aspect of an understanding of spatial politics that I discussed at length with Chris and others in California. First, no element of the social world is neutral. Nothing can be treated as if it just does what it does: all things are partisan toward one vision of a world, one specific reading of it, its histories, and its possible futures. Arguing otherwise is what underpins, for instance, what a logic of austerity measures as "objectively necessary." Second, an attempt to practically change the meaning of those elements, to reverse them and make them not ours but no one's, requires a thick understanding of their history, especially the variant ends for which they were designed and put to. Such an understanding can only be gained collectively, in struggles against whatever declares itself neutral and necessary, and in the networks of care that both support and are created by those struggles.

For example, reading back over our correspondence after his death, I found something Chris sent to a few of us in the fall of 2009, back at the start of the sequence of occupations that marked the year. It's a text he was writing called "Barricades Are Everywhere," one designed to be read interspersed with chants, so that it kept shuttling back and forth between the speaker and the crowd.

Cutting against an easier, if wholly tempting, radical imaginary of the barricade, he points out: "But we are not the only ones who have built barricades. Those in power have been building them for years," whether in Iraq, around Wall Street, surrounding Palestine, or at the G-20. However, he writes,

We do not oppose the use of barricades. Indeed, they are essential for anyone seeking to liberate the spaces currently occupied by power. We are fortunate in that this very tactic of power can be reversed upon the ruling order by those who know how to use it.

In other words, the barricade has never been a neutral thing to be deployed. It is used in moments of rupture and in sequences designed to circumvent and deny them. But if it is not neutral, it is also not wholly determined and stuck in an easy flipping binary of for us or by cops. It requires we open to another problem, a longer one: to understand what all has played the role of cops, what constitutes the full network of the cordon sanitaire, and how we can grasp who and what has been historically excluded by that notion of us, what kinds of policing of our own we've been complicit in. This is a problem that historians like Foucault and Chris struggle with. But historians like them really matter because they know that it can't be answered in works of history. It will be elaborated in struggles over and through the meaning and organization of those objects, sites, and concepts, in efforts that pose those necessary questions: how can hospitals be reorganized to serve those who need them? How do we stop circulation while getting what is needed to sustain that stoppage? (And a less difficult but still important question how do you make a barricade of urinal dividers?)

One of the things I, like a lot of people, took away from studying deconstruction was to challenge easy oppositions of speech and text, and with it, an untroubled sense of presence as the mark of an expressive, identifiable subject. But it was a unique force and generosity of Chris's thought and life that helped me think through this schematic differently, to treat the act of reading as inseparable from an articulation of us all as better antagonists of the present, and that articulation as itself requiring that we attend to the real material force of discourse. How has what's been said and written shaped what's possible? How has what was never said or written done the same? In this, we start to see historical arrangements of revolt and repression, of buggery and blasphemy, as themselves articulating theories of contestation, not just something to be theorized after the fact. Chris reminded me that the work of genealogy is no labor of Enlightenment. It's a process of listening close, above all to those who weren't asked to speak in the first place, to those who insistently made their voices heard all the same. We're all the better for having heard his. ◢

SARAH MESLE (PhD, Northwestern) is faculty at USC and Senior Humanities Editor at the *Los Angeles Review of Books*.

MERVE EMRE is a Visiting Fellow at the American Academy of Arts and Sciences. In 2016, she will be an assistant professor of English at McGill University.

CALEB SMITH is professor of English at Yale University. He is the author of *The Prison and the American Imagination* (Yale University Press, 2009) and *The Oracle and the Curse: A Poetics of Justice from the Revolution to the Civil War* (Harvard University Press, 2013). His essays on contemporary culture have appeared in *BOMB*, *Paper Monument*, *Yale Review*, and Avidly.org. His homepage is http://calebsmith.commons. yale.edu/.

NAMWALI SERPELL is an associate professor of English at UC Berkeley. Her writing has been published in *McSweeney's*, *The Believer*, *Bidoun*, *Callaloo*, *Tin House*, *n+1*, *The Caine Prize Anthology*, and a collection, *Should I Go to Grad School?* (Bloomsbury, 2014). Her first published short story, "Muzungu," was selected for *The Best American Short Stories 2009*, shortlisted for the 2010 Caine Prize for African Literature, and anthologized in *The Uncanny Reader* (St. Martins, 2015). In 2011, she was selected to be one of six recipients of the Rona Jaffe Foundation Writers' Award for women writers. Serpell is currently working on a book of essays, *Losing Face*, and a novel, *The Furrows*.

JULIE KANTOR is a PhD student in American Studies at the University of Texas at Austin. Her poetry has been published in *Boston Review*, *A Public Space*, *Maggy*, and *Foothill*. Her chapbook, *LAND*, was published in July 2015 by Dikembe Press.

MICHAEL W. CLUNE's most recent critical book is *Writing Against Time* (Stanford UP, 2013). His first work of creative nonfiction, *White Out*, was named a Best Book of 2013 by *The New Yorker*, NPR, *The Millions*, and elsewhere. His most recent book is *Gamelife* (2015, Faber & Faber). He teaches at Case Western Reserve University.

DOROTHEA LASKY is the author of four books of poetry, most recently *ROME*. She currently lives in New York City and teaches at Columbia University's School of the Arts.

PETER COVIELLO teaches at the University of Illinois, Chicago. He has written about Walt Whitman, the history of sexuality, queer children, 18th- and 19th-century American literature, Mormon polygamy, and Steely Dan. His most recent book is *Tomorrow's Parties: Sex and the Untimely in Nineteenth-Century America*, a finalist for a 2013 Lambda Literary Award in LGBT Studies.

KATHRYN BOND STOCKTON is Distinguished Professor of English and Associate Vice President for Equity and Diversity at the University of Utah, where she teaches queer theory, theories of race, the 19th-century novel, and 20th-century literature and film. Her most recent books, *Beautiful Bottom, Beautiful Shame: Where "Black" Meets "Queer"* and *The Queer Child, or Growing Sideways in the Twentieth Century*, published by Duke University Press, were both finalists for the Lambda Literary Award in LGBT Studies (2007 and 2010), and she has authored *God Between Their Lips: Desire Between Women in Irigaray, Bronte, and Eliot* (Stanford University Press). Stockton has received the Crompton-Noll Prize, awarded by the Modern Language Association, for the best essay in gay and lesbian studies and, in 2011, she taught at Cornell University's School of Criticism and Theory, where she led a seminar on "Sexuality and Childhood in a Global Frame: Queer Theory and Beyond." In 2013, she was awarded the Rosenblatt Prize for Excellence, the highest honor granted by the University of Utah.

LO KWA MEI-EN is the author of *Yearling* (Alice James Books, 2015), which received the Kundiman Poetry Prize, and *The Bees Make Money in the Lion* (CSU Poetry Center, 2016), winner of the Cleveland State University Poetry Center Open Book Prize. A chapbook, *The Romances*, is forthcoming from The Lettered Streets Press. Recent work can be found in *PEN Poetry Series*, *The Margins*, *The Offing*, and *VIDA: Women in Literary Arts*. She lives and works in Cincinnati, Ohio.

Los Angeles multimedia artist **ANDREA BOWERS**'s work explores the intersection between activism and art. Her intricate photorealist drawings, large-scale graphic works, videos, and ephemera pay homage to a multitude of movements and causes, particularly feminism, climate justice, immigrant rights, and workers' rights. She is a member of the SEIU Local 721 and currently a member of the Bargaining Committee for the Otis College of Art and Design Part-time Faculty Union. She has been teaching in the Otis Graduate Public Practice Program since 2007.

VIRGINIA JACKSON is UCI Endowed Chair in Rhetoric in the departments of English and Comparative Literature at the University of California, Irvine. She is the author of *Dickinson's Misery: A Theory of Lyric Reading* (Princeton: Princeton University Press, 2005) and the co-editor (with Yopie Prins) of *The Lyric Theory Reader: A Critical Anthology* (Baltimore: Johns Hopkins University Press, 2014). Her book *Before Modernism: Nineteenth-Century American Poetry in Public* is forthcoming from Princeton, and she is now at work on *After Poetry*, a book on 21st-century American poetics.

ROBIN COSTE LEWIS is a Provost's Fellow in Poetry and Visual Studies at the University of Southern California. Her poetry collection, *Voyage of the Sable Venus*, will be published by Knopf this fall.

JOHANNA DRUCKER is the inaugural Breslauer Professor of Bibliographical Studies in the Department of Information Studies at UCLA. She is internationally known for her work in the history of graphic design, typography, experimental poetry, fine art, and digital humanities. In addition, she has a reputation as a book artist, and her limited edition works are in special collections and libraries worldwide. Her most recent titles include *SpecLab: Digital Aesthetics and Speculative Computing* (Chicago, 2009) and *Graphic Design History: A Critical Guide* (Pearson, 2008, second edition late 2012). She is currently working on a database memoire, *ALL*, and the online Museum of Writing in collaboration with University College London and King's College, and a letterpress project titled *Stochastic Poetics*. A collaboratively written work, *Digital_Humanities*, with Jeffrey Schnapp, Todd Presner, Peter Lunenfeld, and Anne Burdick is forthcoming from MIT Press.

ANDREW NANCE's poems have recently appeared or are forthcoming in *Colorado Review, Guernica, Gulf Coast, The Literary Review, OmniVerse, Prelude, The Volta*, and elsewhere. He is the editor of Company and lives in Athens, Georgia, where he is currently a PhD candidate at the University of Georgia. Find him online at: andrewnance.org.

KENNETH GOLDSMITH is the author of eight books of poetry, founding editor of the online archive UbuWeb (http://ubu.com), and the editor of *I'll Be Your Mirror: The Selected Andy Warhol Interviews*, which is the basis for an opera, *Trans-Warhol*, which premiered in Geneva in March of 2007. Goldsmith is also the host of a weekly radio show on New York City's WFMU. He teaches writing at the University of Pennsylvania, where he is a senior editor of PennSound, an online poetry archive. More about Goldsmith can be found on his author's page at the University of Buffalo's Electronic Poetry Center: http://epc.buffalo.edu/authors/goldsmith.

DIANA FUSS is Louis W. Fairchild Class of '24 Professor of English at Princeton University. Fuss is the author of *Essentially Speaking* (Routledge, 1989), *Identification Papers* (Routledge, 1995), and *The Sense of an Interior: Four Writers and the Rooms that Shaped Them* (Routledge, 2004). In 2005 *The Sense of an Interior* won the MLA James Russell Lowell Prize for outstanding scholarly book of the year. Her most recent book, *Dying Modern: A Meditation on Elegy*, is forthcoming from Duke University Press. Fuss is also the editor of several volumes: *Human, All Too Human* (Selected Essays of the English Institute), *Pink Freud*, and *Inside/Out*, which won both the *ALA* and *VLS* best book awards.

MARGARET RONDA's book of poems, *Personification*, won the Saturnalia Books Poetry Prize and was published in 2010. Her poems have recently appeared in *AGNI, Aufgabe, Columbia Poetry Review*, and *Gulf Coast*. She teaches American poetry and environmental theory at the University of California, Davis.

KENNETH W. WARREN is Fairfax M. Cone Distinguished Service Professor of English at the University of Chicago.

A former Stegner Fellow at Stanford University, **BRIAN TEARE** is the recipient of poetry fellowships from the National Endowment for the Arts, the MacDowell Colony, the Fund for Poetry, the Marin Headlands Center for the Arts, and the American Antiquarian Society. He is currently a 2015 Pew Fellow in the Arts. He's author of five full-length books, *The Room Where I Was Born, Sight Map*, the Lambda Award–winning *Pleasure*, Kingsley Tufts finalist *Companion Grasses*, and the forthcoming *The Empty Form Goes All the Way to Heaven*. He's also published seven chapbooks, most recently *Paradise Was Typeset, Helplessness, [black sun crown]*, and *SORE EROS*. After over a decade of teaching and writing in the San Francisco Bay Area, he's now an Assistant Professor at Temple University in Philadelphia, where he makes books by hand for his micropress, Albion Books.

JONATHAN FREEDMAN is Professor of English at the University of Michigan.

TAVIA NYONG'O is a cultural critic and an Associate Professor in the Department of Performance Studies at New York University. He writes on art, music, politics, culture, and theory. His first book, *The Amalgamation Waltz: Race, Performance, and the Ruses of Memory* (Minnesota, 2009), won the Errol Hill Award for best book in African American theatre and performance studies. He is completing a study of fabulation in black aesthetics and embarking on another on queer wildness. Nyong'o has published in venues such as *Radical History Review, Criticism, GLQ, TDR, Women & Performance, WSQ, The Nation, Triple Canopy, The New Inquiry*, and *n+1*. He is co-editor of the journal *Social Text* and the Sexual Cultures book series at New York University press. He regularly blogs at *Bully Bloggers*.

EVAN CALDER WILLIAMS is a writer, artist, and translator. He is the author of *Combined and Uneven Apocalypse, Roman Letters*, and, forthcoming, *Against the Flood: The Italian Critique of Gender and Capital* and *Donkey Time*.

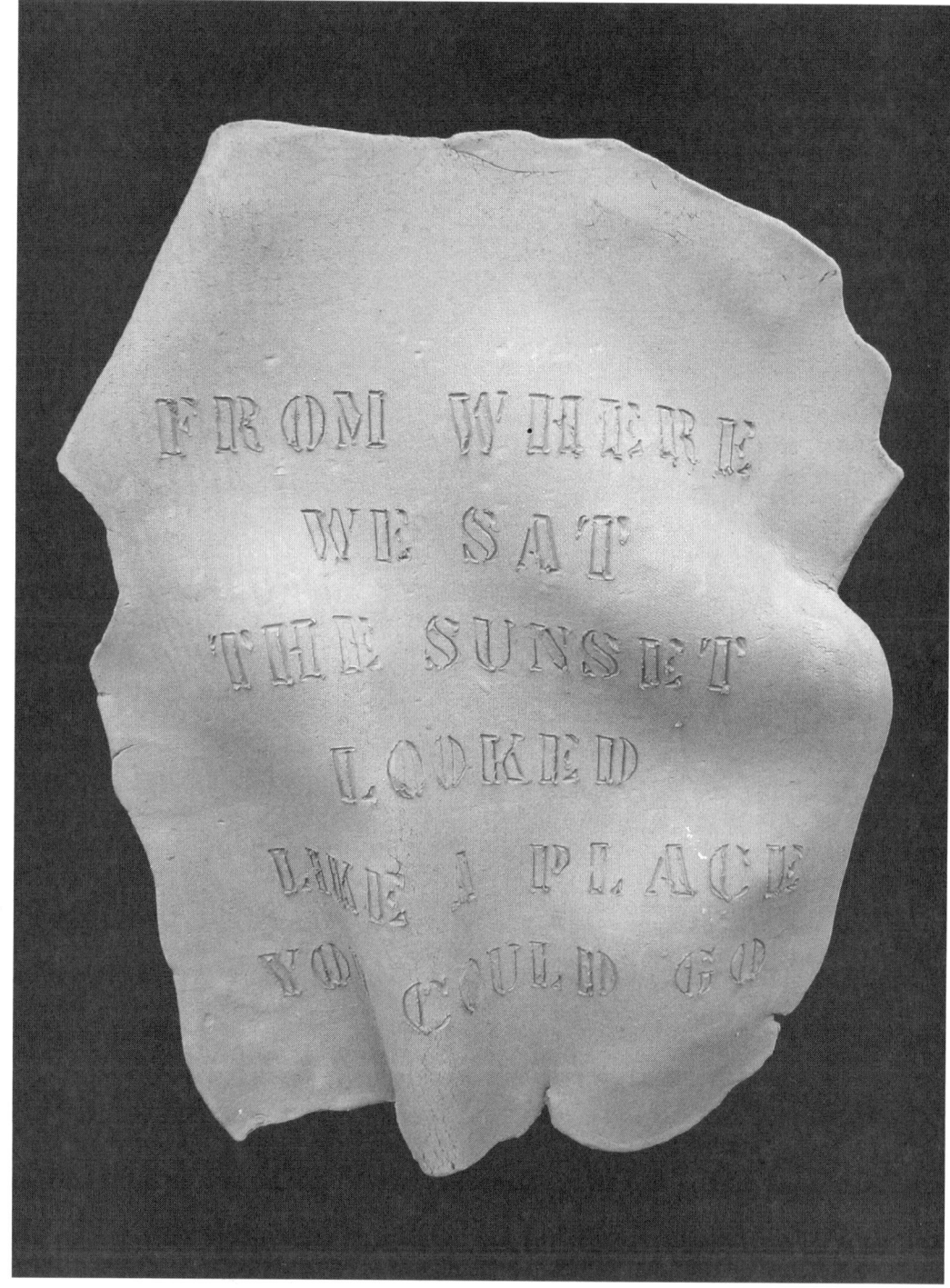

ANNA MAYER
FROM WHERE WE SAT, THE SUNSET LOOKED LIKE A PLACE YOU COULD GO (TEMESCAL CANYON),
FROM THE *FIREFUL OF FEAR* PROJECT, 2008–ONGOING
WILDFIRE-FIRED CERAMIC (FORTHCOMING), 19 x 15 x 3"
COURTESY OF THE ARTIST